NEW YORK SAWED IN HALF

NEW YORK SAWED IN HALF

An Urban Historical

by

Joel Rose

The True Story

of

What May or May Not Have Been

the Greatest Hoax

Ever Played on the Citizens of Gotham

BLOOMSBURY

Published by Bloomsbury Publishing, New York and London
Distributed to the trade by St. Martin's Press

Library of Congress Cataloging-in-Publication Data
Rose, Joel.
New York sawed in half: an urban historical/
by Joel Rose. – 1st US ed.
    p. cm.
'The true story of what may or may not have been the
greatest hoax ever played on the citizens of Gotham.'
ISBN 1-58234-098-6
1. New York (N.Y.) – History – 1775–1865. 2. Manhattan
(New York, N.Y.) – History – 19th century. 3. Impostors and
imposture – New York (State) – New York – History –
19th century. 4. New York (N.Y.) – Social conditions –
19th century. 5. New York (N.Y.) – Biography. I. Title.

F128.44.R67 2001
974.7'103–dc21   00–049844

First U.S. Edition

10 9 8 7 6 5 4 3 2 1

Typeset by Hewer Text Ltd, Edinburgh, Scotland
Printed and bound in the United States of America
by R.R. Donnelley & Sons

To the memory of my father,

Milton Rose

Extremes, in success and defeat, health and disease, wealth and poverty, comfort and misery, plenty and beggary, every day and every where, abound.

Joel Ross, M.D.
What I Saw in New York or
A Bird's Eye View of City Life

Chapter One

In which we are introduced to a retired butcher who says
he and his friend, a carpenter, pulled off the greatest hoax
in the history of New York City.

THE WEATHER HAD JUST TURNED.

It is 1824, possibly 1823.

Thirty-five years later, recounting the story, Uncle John
De Voe, a retired, old-time butcher, talking to his nephew,
Thomas F. De Voe, himself a retired butcher, as well as an
enthusiastic member of the New York Historical Society,
who was writing an all-encompassing book about the markets of the city of New York and the foodstuffs sold therein,
said he could not quite remember for sure which year it was;
he did recall that it was late spring, or early summer, what he
remembered as one of the first really beautiful days of the
year after a particularly brutal winter.

The city had recently struggled through a devastating
economic depression. Food was scarce, work scarcer.

In addition, summer past saw a terrible yellow-fever
epidemic, what had become almost an annual plague, dec-
imate the population. Droves of frightened people had fled
the confines of the city for the wilds of Greenwich Village
and upper Broadway, only returning after the fall chill had
set in and the air had become clear.

To hear Uncle John tell it, he and a friend, a man he
recalled as simply Lozier, proceed down Mulberry Street that

day. They wander into the old Centre Market, housed near the triangle intersection of Centre, Orange (now Baxter), and Grand Streets.

The pair, both getting up there in years, but De Voe somewhat younger than his companion, find their way through the stalls, past the displayed clumps of root vegetables – Long Island potatoes, white turnips, and yellow and red parsnips – the seasonal produce just starting to come in from the country farms, most of it gone this late in the day; what is left, the dregs, the market having been open since early morning.

They peer at the last remnants of what were earlier mounds of flat fish, fluke, and flounder, the bedraggled array of limp blue fish, striped bass, and shad, the few remaining small glistening piles of black and gray shellfish, clams and oysters, dredged locally from the abundant beds of New York Harbor.

They eye the vestige displays of stringy red fat beef in the butcher stalls, the crooked rows of plucked yellow ducklings hanging by their gizzards, the alternating stacked pyramids of brown and white hen eggs, the live turkeys – small, crowded, sad, caged two and three to a crate.

A twelve-year-old girl, smudge-faced and barefoot, in a blue calico dress, tired, carrying a cedar basket by a leather strap around her dirt- and sweat-streaked neck, trudges past them, half singing, half shouting, 'Yams! Hot yams! Get yer hot yeller hot yams! Hot! Hot! Fresh from the pot! Yams! Hot yams! Get yer hot yeller hot yams, and let poor me go home!'

Eventually Lozier and De Voe wind their way to the back

of the market where several crude wooden tables and rough-hewn benches have been set up. Here a group of purveyors: butchers, truck farmers, and fishmongers congregate daily at the end of work to drink and commiserate, gossip, and pass the current news of the day.

The pair find seats, dispatching a dirty eight-year-old boy, dressed in rags, across the street to a local grog shop for a bucket of beer. They have seated themselves off a little bit to one side, perhaps for the purpose of privacy, but after a few beers they seem to invite an audience, and begin to talk loudly enough so that others around cannot help overhearing their discussion. Some among the stall workers think the two men look somewhat familiar.

Their conversation is of a nature that those nearby find it impossible not to take interest and listen in. As a result, the two men are soon joined at their table by a gaggle of curious eavesdroppers, self-invited, eager to hear more and even involve themselves in the discussion, especially because the subject matter evidently involves the shared fate of each and every one of those now pressing close.

And so, in voices deeply colored by concerned, dramatic pauses, heartfelt throat-clearing, and murmurs, the pair proceed on their course, speaking in appropriately somber tones of what is not exactly clear, but some dire and terrible problem nonetheless, that even as they speak, is poised to befall the already oft-deviled island of Manhattan on which they all live.

The older of the pair takes the lead, introduces himself by the single name Lozier. He doesn't offer a Christian name, and none is recorded by history. Uncle John admits Lozier wasn't even his real name, but can't recall, all these years later, he tells his nephew Thomas, what the fellow's real name actually was.

From the look of him, his demeanor, Uncle John recounts, the way he comports himself and commands respect, those working stiffs and hangers-on gathered around assume Lozier is a man to be respected, concluding – and rightfully so – that he is a man well-off, even of some wealth.

Uncle John, the man who some thirty-five years later cannot quite remember the exact year of this incident's occurrence, is an affable fellow of extremely pleasant manner, according to his nephew, and it is he, it turns out, who is the one who seems the more familiar to his and Lozier's audience. He has, as a matter of fact, worked with some of those now gathered around. As said, a retired butcher, he has spent the better part of his life working the major markets of the city of New York, including the Fly, Washington, and Collect markets. He reminds the collected that his name is John De Voe, but explains most folk simply call him 'Uncle John' or even 'Uncle'. He requests that all those assembled about address him just so, no need for anything more formal.

While Uncle John shakes hands all around, renewing dim friendships and acquaintances, Lozier takes the opportunity to explain to those who might not know that he and his colleague, a man of eminence, are lifetime residents of the fair metropolis of New York, but they've been away, dispatched to Washington, D.C., on troubling business, and have only just returned to their native Gotham a few days prior.

Lozier, looking about him as if someone might be listening

4

in on something they should not be hearing, whispers that he and Uncle John have been on this said leave at the behest of none other than the mayor of the City of New York, His Honor Stephen Allen, sent as special emissaries to the nation's capital, where they have now been enlisted as primary consultants to the federal government, answering directly to President James Monroe himself.

An immediate hush goes over the gathered with the mention of the president and Mayor Allen, a wealthy retired sailmaker held in high general esteem.

After a dramatic pause long enough for this information to appropriately sink in and do its work, Lozier goes on to gravely explain his and De Voe's mandate as they see it, the only mandate possible given the extremely dire nature of the circumstances confronting them. Their charter, he announces, his face a serious, tight mask, is to immediately and without hesitation form and implement a radical plan of solid and substantial action to offset the already terrible damage wrought on their island, and prevent disaster, even massive loss of life.

Every man listening feels the eerie tingle and chill of intrigue and terrible fear run down his spine.

What in the name of Heaven and Hell could they be talking about? What so more drastic could possibly befall them after already so much trial and recent tribulation? The faces around Lozier and De Voe have become truly saucer-eyed.

'Hopefully,' Lozier goes on, 'with the Lord on our side, we shall come up with a viable solution before permanent and catastrophic disaster overtakes us all!'

For a long moment all remain silent as the gathered pause to consider what various sorts of imagined calamities and horrors might lay in their future.

Finally one hodman can take the tension no longer and speaks up: 'But what exactly is the nature of this catastrophe?'

'K-K-Kerrect! Of what sort of problem are we sp-sp-speaking here?' stutters a skinny, pockmarked vegetable vender.

Having been waiting for just such encouragement, Lozier takes his cue, and wades in. 'The fact is the population of our island is growing at an extraordinary rate,' he explains with what proves an exceptional knack for melodrama, because this, of course, could not have been more true. Every one knew it to be fact, and no one argued with it. The Catholic Irish were streaming into the city by the packetload, fleeing starvation and more in face of the potato famine on their own native island. The population of the city was nearing 150,000. New York had become, over the last seven or eight years, the biggest, most densely populated city in the country.

'The reality is that in order to accommodate all these people, a huge amount of building is necessarily going on,' Lozier continued.

The hammering and the animated voices of workmen could be heard, right this moment, right where they sat and stood, underscoring the validity of his statement. 'As a result lower Manhattan is becoming entirely too built upon and overburdened.'

This was a point of fact not to be refuted, and had been a recent and recurrent topic of conversation on the benches in this very market, not only this day, but over a period of some time, having been argued and discussed to no real conclusion. The city was overcrowded and dirty, not only filled with hoards of newly arrived poverty-stricken immigrants, but also, to add insult to injury, packs of wandering pigs who had been allowed to take over the streets in the name of public sanitation, nosing their way through mounds of garbage, defecating and procreating at every turn, causing outrage with their oinking ways.

Uncle John told his nephew that at this juncture, he took the opportunity to steal a glance around the table, at each face individually, their wide eyes, their expectant expressions.

'The island is becoming bottom-heavy to an extreme,' Lozier announced, carefully measuring his words to gauge the alarm they might generate on his transfixed audience. 'Toward the southern end at Castle Garden and the Battery, the island is beginning to sink hopelessly into the harbor.'

Some, those of a skeptical bent, here looked at each other, but for the most part, the faces of the others around the small table in the mucky, dirty back of Centre Market were veritable mirrors of confusion and outright worry.

Uncle John explained to his nephew that upon seeing those expressions of distress and calamity, he was much amazed and astonished at how easily the poor, gullible men were immediately taken in.

Taking note, Lozier touched his partner's arm to keep him in check. He was now poised and eager to seize the moment.

'Have no fear,' he continued. 'Mr. De Voe and I are professional men. We are here to afford a solution.'

Lozier announced he had, in fact, sailed the world's oceans a number of times during the course of his working life, which was all true. He was used to problems of every conceivable variation, and used to solving them. Although, he humbly admitted, never quite one of this staggering magnitude or scope.

At any rate, he said, he and his associate, De Voe, had been recruited for just such purpose, to solve this fearful ill that had come to weigh on their beloved city, and as was their duty, they had just about settled upon a plan, after several weeks of intense and careful study, that would surely take care of everything.

De Voe, like everyone else, looked to Lozier. All waited expectantly.

Some of the more vocal shouted, 'What will you do?'

'Our intention is to have Manhattan Island sawed in half' Lozier told them, 'and turn the sawed-off piece down where the Battery is now located.'

There followed an audible gasp.

Lozier went on to say that once the offending bottom-heavy land was cut free, their plan was to tow the severed half out into the harbor, using a system of huge iron stanchions set on Staten Island and Brooklyn, rigged with thick ropes, pulleys, and using strong horse and determined mule teams to pry the land free. Finally, and in addition a phalanx of able-bodied men with extremely long and sturdy oars would coax the severed half away from its mooring.

With that first task accomplished, they would then endeavor to turn the sawed-off bit around and refasten it.

In this described manner the bottom-heavy portion of the

island would become the top, the top half the bottom, and Gotham would, by the will of God, be saved.

The assembled looked at one another incredulously, and then a thin, thirsty oysterman amongst them scratched his head and called out, 'How about another ale?'

A number of boys were sent out. Following the next round of drinks, a long, intense discussion heated up in the ranks, in regard to whether such a task could actually be accomplished.

Lozier assured the assembled that his calculations indicated it indeed could. He said he was staking his reputation on his skill and acumen and was here and now prepared to begin implementation of the plan to saw New York off.

Their first course was to hire the necessary workers.

As Lozier proclaimed, at the very least, a vast army of laborers would be needed, hundreds upon hundreds. Especially in demand would be the sawyers, those skilled craftsmen enough to do the actual cutting. Lozier said these men would need to be especially strong and deft because it would be necessary for them, working in tandem, to wield huge specially built saws.

In addition, a good many pitmen would be needed. These were workers able to go below and do the dirty work of hacking beneath ground, some even eventually proceeding into the brackish water beneath the land so as to do the final amputation.

Ironworkers and ropewalkers would also be in demand. The smithies would be used to forge the huge iron stanchions that would be buried in the earth on the tips of Staten Island and Brooklyn, and on the Battery, so that the long, thickly woven hemp ropes could be secured and teams of horses and mules attached, and the severed section of island pulled loose, floated out, and pivoted.

Also necessary would be a massive anchor to prevent the sawed-off portion from being washed out to sea in case of storm. And oarlocks, huge cast-iron towers in which the gigantic sweeps could be maneuvered.

Of course, it went without saying, dozens of oars would also be needed to help row out the sawed-off part into the harbor. Each oar would need to be some vast size to be effective.

Cooks and provisioneers would be necessary, as well as camp managers to efficiently run the barracks and tent cities that would be used to house the workers. Mule trains, teamsters, and cartmen would be needed, and real-estate organizers to secure the necessary land.

The list went on and on.

Lozier asked whether there would be any volunteers ready to get to work immediately.

De Voe told his nephew that he was shocked to see virtually every hand shoot up.

At Lozier's instruction De Voe took names for a preliminary list, promising to return the next day with a ledger book proper, and with this said, what may, or may not, have been the greatest hoax in New York City history was under way: the mammoth project to saw New York in half.

Chapter Two

In which the reader gets a brief history of Centre Market,
Bunker Hill, animal baiting, the body of water known as
the Collect, and the repercussions of said body on the
surrounding environs, including the political implication
and impact on the people who lived there.

THE LAND OCCUPIED BY CENTRE MARKET, where Lozier and
De Voe purportedly hatched their hoax, once comprised an
expanse of ground owned by the Bayards, a venerable New
York shipping family, and was therefore known popularly as
Bayard's Mount, and sometimes Bunker Hill.

Originally, the top of the rise, situated near what would
eventually become the corner of Mulberry and Grand
Streets, loomed fully one hundred feet over the surrounding
countryside. During revolutionary times, a fort was constructed on this apex, and from here rebel forces fought
valiantly, but unsuccessfully, to resist British troops under
General Howe.

Following the war, the fort remained, although the bones
from the Bayard family burial vault, which occupied the
southeastern side of the hill, were moved, and shortly after
that, what remained of the old burial vault was thrown
down.

For a while the hill found use as a dueling site. The
Monsieur Chevalier de Longchamps was killed here at the
hand of Captain Verdier, a French officer in the Pulaski

Legion, who later that very day set sail for the West Indies rather than face legal and social consequences.

In 1800 the fort was taken over by Samuel Winship, another butcher, a massive man whose weight fluctuated a great deal, generally hovering somewhere in excess of 250 pounds. Despite his huge size, Butcher Winship was reportedly free-hearted and jovial with a genuine love of sport. The sport for which Butcher Winship was most passionate was animal baiting.

Bullbaiting was one of the most popular pastimes of the day. The sport was first introduced in New York in 1763 at the old Delancey Arms tavern on the Bowery, and Bunker Hill soon became a favorite spot for the life-and-death struggle.

Butcher Winship had the idea to build an arena at the top of the mount, selecting to set it directly inside the old Revolutionary War battlement. He constructed a very high board fence, with concentric circles of seating within, surrounding the prescribed bullring. For the pleasure of an afternoon of sport and gambling he charged twenty-five cents admission fee. The simple bench-style circus seating arrangement accommodated two thousand hardily involved enthusiasts. The event was legal, and advertising encouraged full houses.

The animal to be baited, usually a bull, but sometimes a bear or buffalo, was starved for a week or more and then when in a particularly foul mood staked out by a length of chain or thick braided rope to a large iron ring driven into the ground, thus permitting the animal to run about in a large well-worn dirt circle.

The beast was then set upon by a number of ferocious bulldogs, trained, and also starved, for that purpose. A good many of the dogs upon entering the conflict were immediately killed, but sometimes they persevered, although Winship had one favorite prize bull, actually a bison, he kept fighting for some years, housing the animal in relative splendor in the basement of his family residence.

Betting was prevalent, and a major part of the afternoon's festivities. Bets might be on the dogs or the bull or which dog would survive or which would be killed first. Permutations were endless.

Frequently sporting afternoons on Bunker Hill would degenerate into pitched battles among the battalions of idle young men, butcher boys, ruffians, and unaccountable vagabonds. Particularly the Broadway Boys and the Bowery Boys, predecessors to the real criminally involved organized gangs of the city, like the Dead Rabbits and Plug Uglies, would 'fight streets' there on the mount top, throwing stones at one another as they partook in their 'hard battles', sometimes employing fists or sticks, rarely anything more, injuries generally comprising a few bloody noses and bruised shins, before the action was dispatched by the appearance of a few 'leatherheads', so called for the well-shellacked firemen's helmets they wore, or city watchmen.

But by 1802 the prospects of Winship's bullbaiting arena was in decided danger at the hands of forces that wanted to tear down not only the sporting venue, but the very hill itself, and use the cut to fill in the Collect, once the source of most New York City drinking water.

Although the island of Manhattan was laced with numerous springs and creeks, the city had always been plagued with too little potable water to accommodate the population. As a matter of fact, a good many, if not all, of the wells and springs were as near to poison as water could be, infused with runoffs from tanneries, breweries, glue factories, and a staggering array of miserable sanitation practices.

The Collect, or Fresh Water Pond, was a lake, picturesque and lovely, bounded by hills, especially to the west where they rose to some considerable height. Its northern shore washed on White Street, Pearl Street to the south, Mulberry Street on the east, and Elm (Lafayette) Street on the west.

It had a navigable outlet stream at the northern end near where Centre Street intersects with White. This stream flowed north across Broadway at Canal. Here a stone bridge had been built to transverse the creek, which continued along the line of Canal Street, flowing through the marshes of the Lispenard Meadows, and eventually feeding into the Hudson, or North River. On the opposite end, Wreck Brook discharged her waters into the East River, through a stretch of land known as 'the Swamp'.

Fed by underground streams, the lake was called Fresh Water by the first Europeans on the island, or Lime Shell Point, taking its name from the deposit of a great quantity of crushed shells that formed a point on the western shore where a Mahacanni/Lenape Indian village of wigwams jutted out into the water.

The Dutch gave the peaceful spot the name Kalchook, or Kach. This eventually changed to Kolck, or Callech, then Colleck, and finally after the English had wrested control of the island from the Dutch, Collect.

Over the course of years, however, the Collect's fresh sweet water became increasingly unhealthy. For decades maidens and washerwomen came daily to do their laundry. Roperies and tanneries, breweries and assorted other factories sprang up and lined its shore. A powder house was built on an island in the center of the pond in 1747. Prior to that, the spot had been a place of executions and varied other punishment – the convicted meeting their fate hanged, burnt at the stake, or broken at the wheel.

Fish once abounded in the waters of the Collect, bringing fishermen and hunters to the peaceful shores and surrounding woods and cliffs, but eventually the waters became so overfished that the use of nets was prohibited.

In 1732 Anthony Rutgers devised a plan where he would drain the marshes surrounding the Collect, now deeded to him, and build homes on the reclaimed land. He made a cut from Wreck Brook and built a canal leading to the Hudson, but he dug the trench so deep the waters of the Collect drained out to the extent that the fish began to die. Compelled to refill the canal already dug, Rutgers became discouraged and gave up on his plan, and so no one bothered with the area until 1791 when the city made a move to purchase all claims on the waters and land from the Rutgers heirs.

'Rutgers' attempt at drainage had reclaimed a considerable area,' explains author Herbert Asbury in his popular and fanciful social history *The Gangs of New York*, 'and as the population of the city increased and the lower end of the island became more and more crowded, many middle and lower class families began building their homes along the borders of the pond and swamp.'

Now the once pleasant fishing and hunting spot sported the dead bodies of cats, dogs, pigs, and rats, instead of catfish, pickerel, and bass.

By 1784 the area had become developed to the extent that the city set a committee to laying out a plan for a system of streets near the pond, and at the same time tried to induce the local people to undertake a project that would finally drain the now seriously health-threatening body of water by way of a forty-foot canal. Twelve years later, in the summer of 1796, little had been accomplished.

The pond remained in a state of fetid unhealthiness until the middle of October 1802, when Street Commissioner Jacob Brown submitted a report to the city council recommending that the Collect be drained and its adjacent lands filled in once and for all, on the grounds that the befouled waters represented a serious health threat. This, he suggested, would be accomplished by opening a canal through Roosevelt Street all the way to the East River, and in the opposite direction toward the Hudson, effectually draining the pond and land. The city would thus be enabled to recoup some four hundred acres in the centre of the metropolis. The land would be of immense value.

Still nothing was done, and the Collect continued to be a nuisance to the city for four years more, until early on the morning of April 24, 1806, when events would be set in motion that would for ever change the landscape of the city.

On that day, the purser from the British warship *Leander* appeared at the old Fly Market, near the ferry slip on the East River docks. He picked his way through the stalls, bought provisions enough to fill five skiffloads, and made arrangements for the food to be delivered the following day.

The *Leander* was one of three British Royal Navy warships lying in New York coastal waters at the time. A sixty-four-gun frigate, she had been busy stopping coasters in order to root out deserters from the British navy, but just as often seizing any able-bodied seaman the command could get their hands on, including American sailors, some of whom were reportedly carted away waving their American citizenship papers.

With the onset of the Napoleonic Wars, both the British and the French navies had cracked down on neutral shipping, particularly American. Still, both sides desired American goods. American exports boomed, and manufacturing and production increased to meet the demand.

More ships were needed, and therefore, more sailors. Pay increased threefold, from eight dollars a month to twenty-four. This was far more than a British tar would make sailing before the Royal mast. As a results, every English vessel that sailed into New York Harbor left shorthanded as thousands deserted.

British warships like the *Leander* were issued orders to stop all neutral shipping and search the crafts for deserters in order to press them back into immediate service. It was not an unusual occurrence for the *Leander* to hold half a dozen vessels at bay at once.

And so it was that the following day, April 25, late in the afternoon, the American coastal sloop *Richard*, on her way from Brandywine Creek, Pennsylvania, to New York harbor, cruising slowly a quarter mile off the Jersey shore, still two miles south of Sandy Hook, was approached by the British frigate.

The *Leander*, ostensibly searching for deserted Royal Navy seaman, fired a warning cannon shot. The ball splashed into the water some forty yards off the *Richard*'s bow. At that time, an order was issued from the *Leander* to the *Richard* to heave to and stand in the water in preparation for boarding. A second cannon charge was fired to emphasize the demand, this one arching high overhead.

The *Richard* complied immediately.

Nevertheless, a third cannon shot rang out, smashing directly into the ship, and tearing off the head of her helmsman, John Pierce.

Word of the attack spread throughout the city. An angry mob hurried to the wharf near the old Fly market, and there seized two of the purser's boats, already laden with provisions meant for the *Leander*. Three other skiffs had left the dock and were well on their way to Sandy Hook. A swift sloop was sent out to overtake them and bring them back.

Once returned to shore, the food and supplies were quickly unloaded on to ten carts and hauled through the streets to an almshouse for distribution to the poor, accompanied every step of the way by an angry, vocal, ever-growing mob.

The Common Council denounced Pierce's death. His decapitated body was put on display, first on Burling Slip, then at the Tontine Coffee House, precursor to the New York Stock Exchange, and finally at City Hall. Flags around the city flew at half-mast, and church bells tolled. Thousands stood in line to view Pierce's corpse as outrage continued to swell.

Although the crisis was more emphatic in New York, there was little doubt that the country was increasingly drifting into another war with Britain. President Jefferson ordered the *Leander* out of American waters.

As tensions continued to mount, at Jefferson's urging, Congress enacted the Embargo Act three days before Christmas in 1807, outlawing all international shipping to and from American ports.

The consensus was that this drastic action would teach Britain and France once and for all the lesson to honor neutrality.

But in fact, the embargo was a terrible miscalculation and backfired miserably, and New Yorkers took to satirically calling the act 'O Grab Me!' (*embargo* spelled backward), as almost all business in the city came to an immediate halt.

New York was primarily a market town. Exports fell 80 per cent, imports 60, and the city turned gloomy and forlorn as unemployment soared. Wharves stood idle. An estimate of five hundred vessels stood at anchor in harbor, lying useless and rotting. Many decks were stripped, hatches battened down, and ships dismantled. The huge lines of carts waiting for goods that had become a common sight clogging the streets surrounding the docks, all but disappeared and those few cartmen who remained were unemployed. Numerous buildings were bricked up and advertised for sale.

Authorities held more than thirteen hundred debtors in prison, almost half of them for owing sums of less than ten dollars, more than a thousand for debts of less than twenty-five.

Never before had New York City seen suffering on such a

level. The winter of 1807–1808 was a miserable one. The weather cold and stormy, laboring people found themselves in such ill times, they could barely feed, clothe, and warm themselves. Many were on the brink of starvation. Beggars swarmed the streets. Thousands wandered around without clothing, food, or lodging.

In January 1808 sailors led an angry mob through the streets, ending up in City Hall Park, where they demanded bread for their starving families and work for themselves.

The Common Council met in emergency session. A soup kitchen was set up to provide some immediate relief, and within weeks more than six thousand hungry individuals were lining up at the almshouse to receive a ration of a quart of soup, a pound of bread, and three-quarters of a pound of beef, three times a week.

Private charities hurried to coordinate their relief efforts. Forty rich and powerful civic leaders formed the General Committee of the Benevolent Associates for the Relief of the Poor, which in turn established the Assistance Society. Their stated purpose was to dole out food, fuel, and clothing to well-investigated families in need, in exchange for promises of moral improvement through the discipline and faith of religion.

Finally talk of filling in the Collect resurfaced. Work-relief projects were instituted, the hope being to press armies of men into service, at least temporarily. Such projects would serve a dual purpose. The unemployed could be put to work, while simultaneously an end could be put finally to the problem of what was to become of the Collect, the once pristine pond, now nothing more than a diseased garbage dump of putrid, polluted waters.

The street commissioner tacked up signs asking for able-bodied workers to help dig the foundation for the new City Hall and other such laborers to drain marshes and level hills, the earth from the cuts to be used to fill in the Collect.

The hope of the city fathers was soon put forth on flyers strategically located in and about the metropolis:

> Let us fill in the Collect
> and all surrounding marsh land!
>
> And on this new and solid foun-
> dation, let us build residences,
> houses, homes. Let us build the
> framework for a new city, a city
> of hope, of cheer, of well-being,
> of promise, of tenacity.

Albeit the homes built were not destined for those calloused and unfortunate laborers themselves, but for those of the privileged class.

Work on filling in the Collect began at once. The hills to the west of the pond near Broadway were shoveled down to a level, the earth and bedrock used to fill in the pond, and in 1814 Bunker Hill was finally and ignominiously brought down.

When the pond was fully filled, streets laid out and cut through, the reclaimed land Centre Street, formerly Collect Street, ran directly south to north through the center of what was once the most important body of fresh water on the island.

In addition to the landfill, a large open sewer had been dug. Beginning at Pearl Street, it ran through Centre Street to Canal, and then followed the original water path to the river. Effectively this sewer was designed to drain all the surrounding property, and thus appreciably add to the score of usable land and building space.

Over the next few years following the project's conclusion, all congratulated themselves and deemed the work a great success. Respectable families moved into and enjoyed immaculate clapboard homes of more than average charm. One single roundsman saw to the security of the entire neighborhood, and at the southern end, Paradise Square, on a summer evening, was just that – *paradise*!

The land for Centre Market, what was once Bayard's Mount, or Bunker Hill, was purchased in 1817 for a price 'much below its value' by the Common Council on the advice of a committee specifically set up for that purpose.

The cost was five thousand dollars, paid to the owner, Morris Martin. For an additional one thousand dollars, a covered market house was built running along Grand Street, measuring eighty feet by twenty-five.

Fourteen butcher stalls were planned, eventually to grow to eighteen, licensed and occupied for the most part by individuals who had previously kept stands at the old Collect Market, which over the course of time had itself degenerated, and was falling down, becoming filthy and disgusting, sodden, and a magnet for insects. So much so that it was ofttimes derisively called the 'Mosquito Market'.

At first the Collect Market butchers protested moving their established places of business. When the inevitability of the outcome became apparent, however, they petitioned for stands in the new market.

In the end Asa Wesson occupied Stall No. 1, Joseph Blackwell No. 2, and so on. Along with these first two, John Hilliker, Jacob Tier, William Reeves, Stephen Hilliker, John Fash, Thomas Mook, William Bowen, James Simonson, John A. Belar, William Mook, and John Triglar occupied the initial fourteen stalls. Most of these butchers would ultimately become involved in the hoax to saw New York in half.

Thomas Mook, who had occupied Stall No. 7 in the old Mosquito Market, made the first sale of meat out of Stall No.8 in the new market, selling what was said to be a fine steak. It was purchased by Daniel Spader, himself an old butcher from the Washington Market, who resided nearby the new market, on Mulberry not far from Spring.

Besides the butcher stands, the Centre Market had a number of fruit-and-vegetable stalls, and one end of the market bordering Centre and abutting on Broome was set aside half for shellfish, half for scale fish.

Beef sold for twenty-five cents a pound, veal for fifteen to eighteen cents. Small turkeys were a dollar fifty.

For a short time all was well; then disaster struck.

As it turned out, the work done on the Collect was horribly inept. The underground springs, once having fed the pond, were not well-capped or adequately redirected, and the landfill was not firmly or properly tamped down, its soil and rock mixed with common refuse. About 1820 the charming and genteel homes, one by one, began to sink into the imperfectly drained-and-filled pond, springing doors and cracking facades. Water seeped into foundations and filled basements, and noxious vapors began to rise from the swamp, diseases such as cholera and yellow fever seeping upward. Quickly, the well-to-do and middle class abandoned the area, and in their place came Irish immigrants of the lowest class and freed Negroes.

By 1824, with the completion of the Erie Canal nearing, New York was standing at the threshold of a new age. The city was the largest in the United States, on the verge of becoming a full-fledged urban center. New York's recent growth was astonishing. In spite of three years of economic depression following the War of 1812, and the financial panic of 1819, the city's population had increased 30 per cent from nearly 124,000 in 1820 to 167,000 in 1825. More than sixteen hundred new homes were built in the year 1824 alone.

Yet on the lower rungs of society, especially in the neighborhood now known as Five Points, an area just below Centre Market, on what had once been Collect Pond; a place that reeked of desperation, having quickly outstripped even London's Seven Dials as the most horrible and over-populated slum on Earth, the populace stood on desperate and dismally hard times.

After their first day's appearance, Lozier and De Voe did not reappear on the benches at the rear of Centre Market for more than a week, and when they finally did show up again, they were hardly prepared for what had been feverishly fomenting in their absence.

Chapter Three

In which we learn of the mayor's concern regarding the
project to saw New York in half, and his most special,
confidential request of Lozier and De Voe.

BEFORE LOZIER AND DE VOE first appeared at Centre Market,
mostly what was being talked about on the benches among
the butchers and regulars concerned a man named John
Johnson, a reputed shanghaier who ran a boardinghouse on
Front Street, which was frequented by sailors.

On a cold wintry night in March 1824, a man had
appeared at Johnson's door, giving his name as James
Murray, saying he was a sea captain on his way south from
Boston, and asking about the availability of lodging. Johnson
offered the choice of several beds, but Murray declined them
all, confiding that he had a sea chest full of money and was
afraid of his fellow sailors. Johnson graciously told him that
in that case he could stay in the privacy of Johnson's own
private room if he was that worried and would feel more
secure there.

Later that night, after Murray had retired, Johnson stole
back into his quarters and crushed the sea captain's head with
the flat side of a hatchet. He then dragged the body to Cuyler's
Alley, a small passageway leading off Water Street and extending down to the river between Coenties and Old Slips,
where the corpse was soon discovered, and within a few hours,
traced back to Johnson's Front Street rooming house.

Before dawn, Jacob Hays, High Constable of the City of New York, came for Johnson. Hays requested that Johnson accompany him to the rotunda in City Hall Park where, unbeknownst to him, the body of Murray was lying under a sheet. The rotunda, sometimes called the 'Chinese Pagoda', was the site of assorted floggings and hangings, and the atmosphere, justifiably, brought a chill to Johnson.

Hays was a well-known figure about town. Many criminals were stopped in their tracks when they heard uttered the warning 'Beware, Old Hays is after you!'

The head of all New York City police officers, Hays had made his reputation on Bunker Hill, where he had become famous for wading into the fray between warring gangs, knocking the topper (hat) off a particularly ferocious battler with his ash staff, and when the participant went to stoop for it, kicking the man in the rump. In this way, it was said, proceeding from gangster to gangster, he had ended many a melee.

He was appointed Captain of the Watch in 1803, and although he resigned that position, remained head of the police forces for forty years. He was said to have the astonishing ability to tell a criminal from an honest citizen by his physiognomy alone. He was master sleuth of his day, the city's first detective, and given credit for inventing a number of additional police procedures, including the art of shadowing a suspect, and the strong-arm practice of the 'third degree'.

Old Hays was also the first known police officer to confront a murder suspect with his own victim.

When initially questioned, Johnson assiduously denied

the murder of the sea captain Murray. Bearing his suspect no heed, Hays went on with his questioning. He was accustomed to initiating his interrogation with a warning: 'Good citizens will tell the truth,' he would intone, cracking his staff on the wooden floor resoundingly for emphasis.

Murray's body remained covered, and the room in the Chinese Pagoda in City Hall Park was dark and sinister.

Hays suddenly swept the sheet off the corpse. 'Look upon this body!' he ordered Johnson. At the same time, he carefully shone the beam of his lantern on the remains. 'Behold the cold and clammy body of your victim! Have you ever seen this man before?'

Johnson jerked back terrified, and cried out in horror, but Hays, unrelenting, shoved him forward and pressed his head down until the suspect was forced to stare into the clouded eyes of the dead man.

'Murderer!' cried Hays. 'Confess! Now have you ever seen this man before.?'

Johnson broke into sobs. 'Yes, Mr. Hays, I have murdered him,' he bawled.

The trial in the Court of Oyer and Terminer was pure sensation. In front of a packed courtroom, the accused, Johnson, in vain attempt to save himself, now denied having confessed to the crime to Hays, but to no avail. He was quickly convicted.

On the second day of April, dressed in white trimmed with black, he was transported from the Bridewell Prison, in City Hall Park, through Broadway, sitting on his coffin in a cart, to an open field at the corner of Second Avenue and Thirteenth Street. On the gallows, at the nearing prospect of meeting his Maker, he had second thoughts, and again admitted his guilt. He was hanged from a pear tree said to have been planted by Peter Stuyvesant himself, his execution witnessed by fifty thousand people in festive mood, a full one-third of the city's population.

When Lozier and De Voe arrived back at Centre Market following their week's absence, talk of the murder had fallen out of favor, and the one single topic of conversation was sawing Manhattan in half, and the prospects of work the mammoth project would bring.

Lozier and De Voe sidled into the marketplace, found places on the benches, and called for ale, but before they could even adjust their britches and be comfortable, or admire the pretty young woman in calico just passing them by, hawking strawberries out of a willow basket, they were surrounded by as an excitable crew of down-on-their-luck men as one could ever imagine.

Pressed by the shouting and braying rabble begging for their attention and grabbing at their cuffs and sleeves, De Voe said he was much troubled, but Lozier was a cool customer.

They were not only a crazy press of butcher boys and butchers' assistants, but men of every description now, dirty Irish up from the 'P'ernts' (Five Points), Swedish and German immigrants, young brazen sporting men with soaped hair locks, and even knots of surly freed Negroes. The lot of them were in a state of agitation, highly excitable, shouting at Lozier and De Voe from every direction, demanding to know was it true what they had heard, were they all in great peril, was the island going to indeed break off, were they going to be killed, was there really work to be had, and if there was work, where had they been this past week, wanting them to know if there was, as they said, work to be had, they were, one and all, ready, willing, and able to go to it.

De Voe, astonished by the sheer exuberance of what was transpiring in front of him, remained mum, waiting for his partner's response to all this incredible hoopla.

Lozier, a man of clear thought and purpose, took his time in answering the clamorers, however. He cleared his throat, surveyed the eager, pushed them back so that he had some room, demanded order. Only after this was achieved did he lower his voice to a confidential level, as if they were children and he was telling them a secret, informing the gathered sotto voce that he had, in fact, during the course of his absence been in constant audience with the mayor.

Lozier claimed he had not left the man's side in all the time he had been away. They were both, he and the mayor, Lozier announced to the assembled, much stricken with anxious concern in regard to the most correct course of action confronting them. But in the end, the mayor had allowed himself to be convinced that sawing off the island was the best and only solution of any real merit. He and the mayor had, Lozier admitted, inevitably come to loggerheads as to where this sawing must take place. Would they saw mid-isle through miles of hard-packed dirt and bedrock, or rather saw the island further north at King's Bridge and spring it free there.

In Lozier's opinion, King's Bridge was the logical choice the island already pretty much cut by the Spuyten Duyvil, but the mayor had voiced some anxiety, and there had been heated discussion as to whether this was, given the length of the island, truly the best place, because if it was King's Bridge, then there may be a problem of clearance.

Lozier casually took out a clasp knife and cut a plug of tobacco from a black cake. He told the men, 'The mayor's concern, if King's Bridge is the way, how shall the island be turned around, as Long Island appears in the way?' Only continuing after fully working the tobacco plug to his satisfaction in his cheek, Lozier went on, 'I told him some advisors think it can be done without moving Long Island at all,' he said, now spitting out a stream of brown liquid on to the ground between his feet, 'that the bay and harbor are large enough for the island of New York to turn around in; while others insist Long Island must be detached and floated to sea far enough, then anchored until this *grand turn* is made, and then brought back to its former place.'

Lozier admitted there were those he had consulted, men he respected, who were concerned about whether there would indeed be room enough to saw the entire island off and float it about as prescribed, or would the Brooklyn end of Long Island indeed also have to be shorn and floated out to sea in order to provide clearance.

The mayor felt, with strong conviction, that there was not enough room. He was in favor of their first thinking, cutting the island in half at a more southern point, perhaps Fourteenth Street, or at Fortieth Street where the island narrows, or a few blocks north at Turtle Bay. Otherwise, he was as stated worried that Long Island, too, would have to be sawed and Manhattan pulled off its moorings to afford enough space for swinging around, just as Lozier had pointed out, and this undertaking would certainly escalate the project into a realm of finance and hardship the mayor and the city was not yet ready with which to deal.

With a great grin of satisfaction, Lozier announced that in the end, he had been able to convince the mayor, swaying him finally to his way of thinking.

'We shall saw Manhattan off, and we shall saw it off at King's Bridge!' Lozier proclaimed. 'We shall then endeavor to row the island out past Governor's and Ellis Islands, maneuver it around as best we can, and row it back! And we will employ each and every one of you in a job of work for which you are most suited and for which you will be fairly paid.'

The anxious gathered men let out with a mighty hoorah cheer, attracting even more to their ranks.

At the end, before dismissing them with instructions to return the following day, Lozier spoke quietly to the prospective workers, swearing them into his confidence, saying that he was enjoining them into his most inner circle of trust. He wanted the men to understand that the only thing the mayor asked of him, was that His Honor's name be kept out of the daily circumstances of the project. For political reasons which he was sure each and every one of them would understand, the mayor had asked that Lozier and De Voe take charge of the entire undertaking. It would be up to them, and only them, to hire the labor and contract and oversee all the work.

'I have thought long and hard about this undertaking,' Lozier told those pressing in to better hear his words. 'I shall respect the mayor's wishes. The responsibility for such a task is cataclysmic. But in the end, there is no other way. I have agreed and on my honor, I shall, with your help – all of your help – prevent catastrophe from overtaking us and destroying our people and our fair city.' And he peered closely into their open, vulnerable faces, and demanded of them, 'What say you?'

Chapter Four

In which we are given a brief history of markets in New York City, the foods sold therein, including those native to the surrounding farmlands and countryside, and witness what the promise of work will do for the average individual of limited prospect.

NEXT DAY, when Lozier and De Voe returned to Centre Market, Uncle John was carrying a large green cloth-covered ledger book under his arm.

During the interview with his nephew, he confessed that he was astonished to find upon his return such a multitude of the poor and unemployed so eagerly awaiting him, all demanding to have their names recorded in the big book of employment.

It was late morning, he recalled, after eleven. Market started early, and, for the most part, was over by ten A.M. The butchers – in top hats, tailed coats, neck cloths, vests, and long white aprons – cut and dressed their meat at home.

The meat was generally transported to market by the individual butchers in a wheelbarrow. Very few kept horse and cart in those days, only those who were doing a large business or lived far away.

A butcher brought to market each day only what he expected to sell. He arrived usually an hour or two before dawn, ready for customers who made it a practice to come to market early each day to have their choice of cuts. The chefs from the best restaurants, the cooks from the wealthiest families showed up shortly after the butchers, their lists in hand, ready to buy up the most desirable meats, produce, fruit, and vegetables. Within a few hours all the best was gone, and the market for all intents and purposes was over. The only ones remaining were the poor and miserly who would come late or lurk about looking for bargains or to pick up remnants.

Bad weather – that is hot weather – was a curse to the market, there being no refrigeration to keep meat from spoiling, nor would there be until 1835, although a farmer by the name of Thomas Moore from Maryland was said to have invented a refrigerator quite a few years earlier, using one conductor, several nonconductors, and several pounds of ice for the purpose of carrying his butter to market in hot weather.

In order to attract customers on some occasions, a steer was paraded through the streets and the butcher's intent to slaughter the animal announced in the newspapers. The following advertisement appeared in the *Daily Gazette:*

EXTRAORDINARY!
To All Lovers of Fat Beef –

This is to inform the public that there will be offered for sale, by Joseph Blackwell and Jeremiah Tier, at No. 1 and No. 11 of the Collect Market near the Circus in Broadway, beef of the most superior quality ever offered for sale in this city. This steer is only six years old, and it is allowed by old experienced butchers will weigh eighteen hundred pounds, and have more fat than any beast has ever produced in the United States.

Meat, fish, and produce were available in the markets seven days a week, but butchers held sway over all other purveyors, and, although there was a shiftless lot devoid of principle or honor, known as 'shark', or 'shirk', butchers, only those butchers licensed were legally allowed to sell at the market.

The Common Council was the legislative branch of the city government, presiding over almost all aspects of commerce and public life in the city, even setting bread prices, and monitoring strangers, and it was they who issued the much-sought-after butcher licenses, leading often to graft and corruption, but always to expense. In 1825 four stalls in the Essex Market sold for $1,790.

The sitting council was made up of one alderman from each of the city's twelve wards, the city recorder, and the mayor, who after 1821 was appointed by the council and served only a one-year term.

It was up to the Common Council to recommend sites for new markets, and there had been more than forty within the city's limits, 'although several have been found located on or near the same spot where a former one had ceased to exist,' according to Thomas De Voe.

Following the first arrival of Europeans on the shores of Manhattan Island, most farmers concentrated on tobacco, and food shortages were commonplace and often devastating.

Sometimes farmers and Indians would venture in from the countryside, selling corn and fish.

Cattle were soon imported from Holland, and later from England, along with hogs, sheep, and goats. Domestic fowls were abundant: wild turkeys, capons, geese, ducks, and pigeons.

From the start, game was plentiful. The Dutch historian Van der Donk, who in the seventeenth century recorded a long and lush inventory of foods available in the New World, claimed the Indians ate not only deer and rabbit, but bear is well, allowing he himself never indulged in the meat, although soberly reporting, 'Several Christians who have eaten bear flesh say it is as good as any swine's flesh or pork can be.'

Local waters yielded an abundance of oysters, crabs, mussels, shrimps, and tortoises. All of which, Van der Donk observed, make fine food.

'Some of the larger oysters produce pearls, but pearls of a brown color. And these are not valuable,' he laments.

'All the waters of the region are rich with sea food. Sturgeons are plentiful, but the fish are not held in high regard, and the roe from which the costly caviar is prepared,' he marvels, 'are cast away.

'Salmon are plentiful in some rivers, striped bass in all the rivers and bays of the sea. Lobsters are plenty in many places. Some of those are very large, being from five to six feet in length, but those best for the table are between one foot and a foot and a half.'

The Dutch planted apple and pear trees, which thrived in the region, as well as peaches, apricots, plums, almonds, persimmons, and figs, and Van der Donk the historian goes on to catalog a dizzying cornucopia of salads, herbs, nuts, vegetables, and fruits, including cabbages, beets, endive, succory, fennel, sorrel, dill, spinach, radishes, parsley, chervil, watercress, leeks, laurel, artichokes, asparagus, cucumbers, calabashes, turnips, pumpkins, squash, Spanish pork (melons), water-citron (watermelon), rosemary, lavender, hyssop, thyme, sage, marjoram, holy onions, wormwood, chives, clary, pimpernel, dragon's blood, tarragon, beans, Indian corn, wheat, rye, barley, oats, peas, flax, hemp, acorns, chestnuts, beechnuts, walnuts, butternuts, hazelnuts, mulberries, cherries, currants, gooseberries, blackberries, raspberries, cranberries, and strawberries.

The first public market in the city opened in 1656 along the Strand, the name given to a strip of land bordering the East River shore, and extended from Broad to Whitehall Street east of Pearl. Here country folk arrived from their farms on a designated market day to sell produce and meat, while livestock was brought to a separate fair twice a year for sale or barter.

The Broadway Shambles, the first market dedicated exclusively to the sale of meat of large animals, was built on the plain outside Fort Amsterdam, the present site of Bowling Green, two years later in 1658.

Twelve butchers were sworn here, and were exclusively empowered to slaughter all cattle consumed within the city's jurisdiction. Any person who had cow or ox to be butchered, or any large animal, was obliged to pay one of these twelve the price of five guilders, or the equivalent of two dollars. A sheep, a goat, a calf, set one back forty cents.

Admitted to this first rank of city butchers were: Egbert Meinderzen, Pieter Jansen, Gerrit Jansen Roos, Paulus Van de Beeck, Jan Van Harlaem, and Asser Levy, who was identified as a 'Jew butcher', and immediately requested to be excused from killing hogs, as his religion did not allow him to do it.

This original lot proved to be a jealous, peevish group, and were from the beginning in court constantly suing, and being sued. Only three days after the Shambles opened for the first time, Egbert Meinderzen was taken in front of the court 'by persons bringing meat to market' who were obliged to pay him tribute in the form of bribes before he would do his sworn butchering duty.

'By the early nineteenth century New York was primarily a marketplace,' observes Luc Sante in his book, *Low Life: Lures and Snares of Old New York*. 'Despite the prevalent pieties about the virtues of home life, only the few streets inhabited by the upper bourgeoisie were solely residential, and these often just temporarily so.'

Butchers held sway in virtually all the city's markets. Yet more and more frequently, the butcher's apprentice was called upon to carry home the purchases of customers, although some thought such practice frivolous.

Uncle John recalled one customer of his at Washington Market, Dr. Samuel Mitchell, voicing the opinion that 'the man who is ashamed to carry home his dinner from market, did not deserve any'.

Dr. Mitchell lived on White Street near Broadway, and carried home each day a well-filled basket in one hand, with a large fish or cut of meat in the other, to balance his load.

Despite the doctor's sentiment, people very quickly came to rely on the butcher to provide someone to carry home all their purchases, and after that it took two or three men standing around the stall, and the same number of boys, to carry basket upon basket of vegetables, poultry, fish, and eggs, arrange them, and send them to the patron's home in proper order.

As he related the experience to his nephew, Uncle John complained that this turned into a source of some anxiety among certain butchers, many of whom spent more time worrying about deliveries than the sale of meat.

'If the [delivery] boy loses a head of salad, breaks an egg, or an apple gone,' he grumbled to his nephew during the course of his interview, 'the master butcher is called upon to account for it, and very likely a scolding with it!'

In almost every well-tended public market, there were stands for the sale of coffee, cakes, and other sweets.

Sometimes a weary vender would wander through the stalls pushing a wheelbarrow, often with a charcoal furnace in it. Here in his makeshift warming oven, he would keep an ample supply of hot gingerbread, and later on in the season, with the arrival of new cornmeal, he would come with cornmeal pudding and cream.

Baked pears were a favorite, swimming in homemade syrup. As was apple cider: 'Sweet cider! Sweet cider! 'Tis equalized to wine, yet people call it cider!'

Every price was haggled over, and it wasn't until much later in the century when John Wanamaker set prices in his department store that prices were labeled on items and set, and then the reaction was immediate and the practice took hold like wildfire.

Opportunity for good eating should have been everywhere. Yet for most of the population, everything so abundant and available was also unaffordable, the diet of the urban poor remaining reprehensible, largely limited to bread, potatoes, corn, peas, beans, cabbage, all washed down by swill milk from cows fed on the by-products of local breweries, and often, in these unpasteurized times, bringing illness and death to children. In good times the poor might get to add a bit of meat, some salt, cheese, butter, sugar, coffee, and tea.

Destitute widows and young children in patched clothing roamed the streets, hawking odds and ends, fruits and vegetables, bits of candy and cakes.

To the left and right of De Voe, summer produce was stacked in pyramids. Apples, peaches, melons, beans, peas. New potatoes ferried in from Long Island, onions, scallions, cauliflower, cherries from upstate, asparagus, squash, corn, celery, spinach, dill, parsley, mint, endive, cucumbers, blackberries, huckleberries.

Off to one side a huckster, an unauthorized purveyor, was hawking smashed berries, only good for jam, their juice staining his white apron.

Around the fish stalls, nasty, aggressive gulls were squawking as they swooped down and viciously pecked at the street, trying to dislodge fish heads and guts where they were tramped into the cobblestones. The scale-fish tables, from whence the smashed chum came, were laid out with what was left from the morning's blue fish, red snapper, striped bass, flatties, porgies, sturgeon, and shad.

As the men waited their turn for De Voe's attention, an argument broke out in front of them between a forestaller and a customer, and that put De Voe in mind of a story, as any number of small events or incidents were likely to do, him being a talkative fellow, and he took out his handkerchief and wiped his brow, as it was a hot day, and put down his pen, and told it, or so he told his nephew.

It seems in his days as a butcher, De Voe had had his stall at Washington Market, and one day a forestaller, who was known as an ornery cuss and a close shaver, in other words, a cheater of his customers, brought a kettle of butter he had bought off a farmer into the market, handsomely done up in pound rolls. This was at a time, according to De Voe, when butter was scarce, and the forestaller had bought it cheaply, but unbeknownst to his prospective customers, he had also systematically scanted the weight, that is, shorted each roll.

Forestallers had a long tradition. They were rogues who made practice of intercepting poor, simple country farmers, or 'strangers', on their way to market. They would paint a dire picture of the problems these strangers would face with their perishable goods once they got to market and play on the farmers' need of a means to sell their produce. The forestallers would buy from the farmers for a cheap price, and once to market sell for a large profit, having increased prices markedly, and thus making it even harder for the poor to survive or even eat.

Unexpectedly the weigh-master saw the forestaller with the farmer's handsome butter opened for sale, and prepared his test scale to weigh it; while doing so, the forestaller in his anxiety, 'quick as thought', slipped a gold coin out of his vest pocket and while the weigh-master's back was turned, thrust it into the top roll, as he thought unperceived by anyone. The roll was taken up, and it weighed full weight, which satisfied the weigh-master without weighing any other; but while he was putting up his scale, a Quaker gentleman, who had been standing off a little distance, and had seen the whole transaction, came up and inquired the price of the forestaller's butter. He was told fifteen pence, which was expensive, but he said, 'Put me that roll in my kettle,' pointing to the roll with the golden coin hidden inside.

The forestaller tried to steer him to another. 'I have that roll sold to a friend,' he said.

'No,' said the Quaker, 'thee has not – thee can give thy friend another roll, if they are all good and weigh alike.' And he turned for support to the weigh-master who said to the forestaller, 'He was entitled to the roll, or any roll he chooses to take, if they are all priced to him.'

With this, the Quaker took up the butter roll and placed it in his kettle, then laid down fifteen pence; and as he was going, he coolly told the forestaller, 'Thee, my friend, will not find cheating always profitable.'

De Voe burst into laughter. But then one in line, with his own high anxiety and little patience, spoke out for him to get back to the business at hand. De Voe pursed his lips, looked once more upon the line of anxious men, and set to.

And so they stood expectantly in line – apprentices, sporting youths, jack tars, soaplocks, bogbusters, freed Negroes – in one single file, in the late afternoon sun, one following the next, waiting their turn.

De Voe perched on a high stool in front of a clerk's high desk, his narrow green ledger book open in front of him, his steel pen poised, as he listened to the name, and then inscribed it, with address, age, and the man's specialty, if any.

The line moved forward, their number growing larger as

word spread that work was to be had, some not even knowing work for what, waiting to have their name written down, inscribed for them in what very well may turn out to be, at least temporarily, the Book of Life.

Chapter Five

In which Lozier takes his band of recruits on a walking
tour so that they can see for themselves firsthand the fact
that the New York island is sinking into the harbor.

FOR THE REMAINDER OF THE DAY, the long line of prospective
workers waited patiently as butchers and fruit-and-vegetable
venders, country folk, and assorted hucksters looked on from
their stalls with ever-increasing curiosity.

De Voe took names till well into early evening.

By next morning even more poor and unemployed were
waiting.

Word had spread among the downtrodden. Now for the
most part, those in line were the newly arrived, the latest
wave of immigrants, Irish and Welsh, washed up on the New
York shore, having heard at home of jobs to be done in
America, the canals and roads to be built, fleeing their own
poverty, their own starvation, not knowing they were just
the beginning of a tidal flood still to come, ready to say
anything in the hopes of employment.

In *Martin Chuzzlewit*, his acerbic novel about America,
Charles Dickens describes their kind, those lined up nose to
back, waiting in front of De Voe, ready to say anything to
gain a job of work: 'There they were,' Dickens writes.
'Farmers who had never seen a plough; woodmen who
had never used an axe; builders who couldn't make a
box; cast out of their own land, with not a hand to aid

them: newly come into an unknown world, children in helplessness, but men in wants, with younger children at their back, to love or die as it might happen!'

None among them daring to think about or question the feasibility of such an undertaking. Was Manhattan really sinking in the harbor? Could the island really break off? Could all those people be killed? Could they themselves be killed? Could an island really be sawed off? Did any of it really make sense?

Finally one surly butcher, after much blowing and huffing and puffing and heated discussion with his fellows, comes forward, shooting De Voe a withering look, mocking and scoffing at Lozier.

Lozier stepping into the breach, scoffing back, remaining undaunted.

The long line of prospective workers take note, but continue to wait their turn, as the curious look on from their stalls, intrigued.

Lozier tells the Irish, the Welsh, the Negroes who have joined their ranks, 'The scope – the scope of this project, the magnificent magnificence.'

After all, if the Erie Canal can be engineered, if such a project is possible, if it's possible for an army of men, like these waiting in line in front of him, to dig a river through the Appalachian mountains from the village of Buffalo to Albany, then what's a little simple sawing off of a mere island? 'Of course it can be done,' Lozier assures them, looking at his skeptic with disdain. 'Of course it can be accomplished. Possible? Indeed!'

No one knew the answer for sure. It wasn't even remotely

their business. Therefore, it was possible. Had to be possible. Their desperation was at such a level. Hadn't the canal once been said to be an impossibility by almost everyone with an opinion, and certainly by a majority of engineers? And who would have thought a steam engine could power a huge oceangoing vessel across the waters to Europe, and isn't it so?

Lozier stood to his height, refused to allow doubt to enter the equation. He puffed his chest like a bantam rooster, albeit an old one, and reminded them he was in the business of hiring a crew, and that's what he was engaged in doing. 'Nothing has improved,' he told the men. 'Look about us! Open your eyes. How many just like you immigrants are streaming into the city? Building is going forward at the speed of Jack Robinson. With all the added weight, this island of Manhattan is daily sinking into the harbor. It could break off anytime now. We are all in peril!'

But if derision threatened, he would enlist the skeptics and everyone else he could muster into a convoy and lead them on a walking tour from their place in the market, down Centre Street, across the open sewer of Canal, via the stone bridge at Broadway, south past Leonard, past Chambers to the magnificence of the new City Hall.

City Hall, designed by John McComb, Jr., and Joseph Francois Mangin, the cornerstone laid in 1803, but the edifice in its entirety not finished until 1812, was part of the same work-relief project that had brought down Bunker Hill and filled the Collect.

Situated in a park like setting, the front and sides were made of white marble, quarried in Stockbridge, Massachusetts, but the back of the building was made from plain local brownstone after the Board of Supervisors, in their wisdom, overruled the architect, arguing that the building was situated so far uptown that the city would never possibly extend beyond the present northern boundary, City Hall Park, and no one would ever see or have interest in the rear anyway. 'It would not attract much notice from the scattered inhabitants who might reside above Chambers Street.'

Still and all, the building boasted spectacular views of the surrounding countryside from the cupola of its rotunda.

So here Lozier called his procession to a halt, and gathered his troops around to prove his point, with not a few casual and curious observers having swelled their ranks.

'Now,' said he, when the lot of them had quieted and settled down, and he had all eyes turned toward him, 'what is it you observe?' He then offered his 'proof', and the proof cited by him was the majesty of the new City Hall and the fact that if one were to stand on the steps of that illustrious building as they were now doing and gaze southward, what did they see?

The assembled turned and gazed as instructed to where Lozier had indicated when he asked them to apprise the situation as they saw it. They then turned back to their stalwarts and fellows. Some said 'the City Hall Park', or 'the New York Hotel'; others, this or that, but these were not the responses Lozier meant to elicit.

'Are we peering upward or downward when we gaze from where we stand down to the Battery?' asked Lozier

'We look down,' one meek voice ventured.

'Exactly!' Lozier replied at a shout, clapping his hands together with approval. 'We look down! We look down! Say no more,' he chortled, swelling his lungs once more with the smug knowledge of certitude. 'We look down. We look down, down, down!' And there was not an individual present there that day on the white marble steps of City Hall who would not agree with him that he or she was looking downhill.

'We look down! Down, down, down into the depths. Never was it like this before.' No one argued, because, in fact, not a person among them actually knew or could recall was it downhill before, from City Hall to the Battery, or not.

'Our island is sinking,' Lozier cried. 'There is no debate and not an inkling of doubt. We are in danger of breaking off. And our prescribed task, gentlemen, is to act before it is too late and real and permanent disaster strikes. To refute our observations now is to deny scientific fact, to bury our heads in the sand, no different from the ostrich. It will do us no good, and in the end, if we chose to ignore, will surely be our undoing. Act while we can, and we shall accomplish a great thing. We shall save our homes, and the homes of our fellow citizens, and our fellows in the future. We shall save our very lives. We shall be heroes. But, more important, we shall put you all to work and you will all work hard, and you will all make money!'

Chapter Six

In which we learn of the art of the hoax, and the climate in Gotham in regard to the art thereof, and ruminate on an essay written by Edgar A. Poe, and wonder how Poe's treatise may apply to our Lozier, and to our De Voe.

THE HOAX, the humbug, the fraud, the ruse, the prank. Looking back over some thirty-five years, John De Voe, while sitting for his interview with his nephew Thomas, recalled the sawing in half of Manhattan as a hoax of some immense proportion, perhaps even the greatest hoax ever pulled off in the City of New York.

P. T. Barnum, arguably America's preeminent perpetrator of the calculated ruse, thought of Gotham as the 'Epicenter of Deception'. For Barnum, the hoax was everywhere in New York.

'The common man, no matter how sharp and tough, actually enjoys having the wool pulled over his eyes, and makes it easier for the puller,' he said.

Or as a more obscure profiteer of the day saw fit to remark, 'I tell you everybody likes to be humbugged, though there ain't many as'll acknowledge it.'

As originally passed, Lozier's remark, in reference to the island breaking off and sinking into the harbor, was tossed off by him as something less than fact, according to Uncle John. A rather innocuous joke, but typically dry. A typical quip out of the typically smart, dry mouth of the smart, and assuredly dry, Lozier. But when his wry attempt at humor was taken for reality, Lozier went with it full bore, just to have some fun and see how far it would carry.

'Among the butchers in the market there were always several "regular jokers", Lozier among them, who were full of life and fun,' Uncle John half reminisced, half lamented to his nephew, 'and fun they be sure to have, sometimes at considerable cost.'

Edgar Allan Poe in 1844 wrote an essay entitled 'Diddling Considered as One of the Exact Sciences' for the *Broadway Journal*. This work provides us with some possible insight into the mind and motivation of a man like Lozier.

Assuredly not one of Poe's greatest works, the title is taken from the fictional name Jeremy Diddler, the protagonist's name in James Kenney's 1803 farce *Raising the Wind*.

'Diddling Considered as one of the Exact Sciences' catalogs the various dodges of cheats; how to get something for nothing, a discursive on dishonesty, but a dishonesty couched in cleverness, and, to some degree, fun.

The definition of the verb *diddle* is 'to cheat or swindle'. Jeremy Diddler is described by the *Oxford Companion to English Literature* as a dawdling swindler. The etymology of *diddle*, according to the *Oxford English Dictionary*, is traceable to the Old English *dydrian*, 'to delude, deceive, to victimize.' A diddler, therefore, may be defined as the perpetrator of a hoax, and Poe, in his rumination, makes attempt to pay homage to the skill and bravado of that individual, the author taking 'delight' in the deception of his fellow man, his weakness, his mystification, his ignorance.

Here, according to Poe's biographer, Hervey Allen, in

Israfel: The Life and Times of Edgar Allan Poe, is one of the most elaborate of Poe's never-very-successful attempts to be funny.

'Poe derived considerable amusement from the distress and surprise of those despoiled,' writes Allen. 'The petty crooks and scoundrels of the story are the heroes, and the laugh is supposed to come when the victim discovers his loss.'

Allen concludes, 'There is a curious parallel between this effusion and Poe's childish and almost unbalanced delight in a hoax of any kind. Such imaginings helped his [Poe's] sense of inferiority, and allowed him a laugh all by himself.'

Poe claims man was born to the hoax, and the hoaxer to the diddle.

'But others find it hard to join in the mirth,' counters Hervey Allen, 'because the writer seems to take an unholy joy in the weakness and the ignorance of his fellow men. There is too sardonic a gusto about it all.'

'Your diddler is minute,' Poe writes in his essay. 'Your diddler is guided by self-interest. Your diddler perseveres.

'Your diddler is ingenious. He has constructiveness large. He understands plot. He invents and circumvents . . . Were he not a diddler, he would be a maker of patent rat-traps or an angler for trout.

'Your diddler is audacious. He is a bold man. He carries the war into Africa. He conquers all by assault.

'Your diddler is nonchalant. He is not at all nervous. He never had any nerves. He is never seduced into a flurry. He is never put out – unless put out of doors. He is cool – cool as a cucumber. He is calm. He is easy – easy as an old glove.

'Your diddler is impertinent. He swaggers. He sets his arms akimbo. He thrusts his hands in his trousers' pockets. He sneers in your face. He treads on your corns. He eats your dinner, he drinks your wine, he borrows your money, he pulls your nose, he kicks your poodle, and he kisses your wife.

'Your true diddler winds up all with a grin. But this nobody sees but himself. He grins when his daily work is done – when his allotted labors are accomplished – at night in his own closet, and altogether for his own private entertainment. He goes home. He locks his door. He divests himself of his clothes. He puts out his candle. He gets into bed. He places his head upon the pillow. All this done, and your diddler *grins*. This is no hypothesis. It is a matter of course. I reason *a priori*, and a diddle would be no diddle without a grin.'

Chapter Seven

In which we continue to hear of the long lines of prospective workers waiting, are given an explanation why these men were so desperate for work of any kind, as more and more free Negroes join the ranks of prospective workers, and we learn of the climate toward them in the city, and the roots of their desperation.

ALL HIRING WOULD BE MADE pending a rigorous fitness examination. Lozier was clear on this aspect, even adamant. The labor involved was of a nature that involved a great deal of physical strength, and it would not do for someone vulnerable to be given a job of work that he was not able to see to completion at risk to his own health and ultimately the project.

Work at the time was not plentiful, especially among the wretched poor, the immigrants who were flowing into the city, and free Negroes.

No matter what the newly arrived had heard in their own suffering countries about the opportunities afforded by the Erie Canal and the national highway connecting Baltimore with the Ohio River Valley, once they got here it was another story. The work crew on the Erie Canal, mostly Irish and Welsh bogbusters, was making great strides forward under the most horrendous of conditions and backbreaking work, this was true, but the Canal Commission was no longer looking for more hirees. Rather, those on the job were so thankful to have any employment that they were working twice as hard, through merciless conditions and disease, so that they were not dismissed in favor of some other dejected fellow just as hungry, if not hungrier, than the poor soul he replaced.

So the lines were long and snakelike at Centre Market, and high on his perch, De Voe had soon penciled more than three hundred names in his huge green ledger book.

Far from being a city of equals, New York was a city based along class lines, and the class lines were hardened with the increasing press of incoming immigrants.

Before and after the War of 1812, panics and depressions set the tone for the economy, which was in the hands of bankers and merchants, speculators and landlords, all of whom were growing rich. It was government by the privileged – the lower class and middle class governed by the upper class.

The average worker was taken advantage of at every turn. He worked, struggled, all for the smallest possible reward. He enjoyed little of the comforts of life, while his employer grew rich off his back. Neglect, poverty, starvation, vice, disease were the watchwords. Bread, meat, rent, and fuel the concerns of every day.

One-third of all workers in the city were out of work at the time De Voe and Lozier made their appearance, and nearly half the population was living in interminable hopelessness and duress. Half of school-age children were not in school. The seeping, fetid landfill of the Collect continued to swallow up houses and give forth miasmic vapors. The rich had long since abandoned the crooked streets and lanes in the Five Points, and the neighborhood was well on its way to devouring its new residents, the city's poor, her Negroes, her foreigners.

In 1818 twenty thousand Irish sailed into New York Harbor, lured by rumors of plentiful work on canals and roads. Most were traveling alone, leaving their families behind until they could sufficiently establish themselves, and by the time they had docked in the New York waterfront, they were stone broke.

It would only be a short time before huge, murderous street gangs would be running rampant through the miserable slums, and the poor would be relegated to the streets like the garbage and marauding pigs used for sanitation.

Almshouses and debtors' prisons overflowed as did grogshops and other establishments where spirits, mostly rum, were sold without a license. Within the city's relatively small confines, taverns numbered six hundred, not even counting assorted tippling shops, wine shops, rum shops, and breweries.

Meanwhile, the streets of the city were becoming progressively more dirty and stinking. Only Broadway, which in 1824 was just getting the first gas street lamps, was cleaned with any regularity. All other streets were swept once a month, if that. The carcasses of dead cats and dogs, rats and mice lay in the gutter, while people threw their ashes and dirt into the streets. The rich grew indignant with what they saw, blaming drunkenness and lack of godliness for all the public ills plaguing the poor.

For some days as the hiring continued apace, Lozier sat on the wooden bench outside Centre Market, watching his handiwork in action, conversing, answering questions, pontificating to any number of the curious who took the seat next to him, while De Voe maintained his position perched on his stool at his high desk, recording names, and the job the man in front of him meant to have.

Word had been rapidly spreading, and now those immigrants in line were joined by more and more free Negroes, as before there had been only a sprinkling.

At the end of the day, a butcher named Jacob Tier, who had the reputation for being a 'tough old bird' and sometimes worked with his son out of Stall No. 5, came and sat with Lozier. They called for a boy and sent him for a bucket of beer.

Soon they were joined by De Voe, and the conversation turned to the great many Negroes who had joined the ranks of prospective laborers signing on for the project.

Tier grumbled about them and made some not flattering remarks. The man was well-known to De Voe, although not to Lozier; retired now, he had first worked out of Stall No. 8 at the Old Swago (Oswego) Market at Broadway and Maiden Lane, and then the old Collect Market, and when that dilapidated place had been condemned, came over here to the new Centre Market, where he had been one of the first to sign on, and at present helped out his son, also named Jacob.

Tier, Sr. was not much given to talking about himself, but as the conversation turned to King's Bridge where Lozier had decided the major sawing was to commence, De Voe, a fount of information and gossip, eagerly told Lozier, with not a small amount of glee, how once, some years back, on a bet,

Tier, a man renowned for his great strength, endurance, and fearlessness, had undertaken to push his butcher's wheelbarrow from his home at the corner of Bowery Lane and Grand Street all the way to Spuyten Duyvil. He won the wager easily, De Voe told Lozier.

There were still a great many Negroes milling through the market, scavenging the day's leftovers, and looking for last-minute bargains.

Tier watched them, and spitting on the ground, he wondered if Lozier was wise to allow these Negroes to work on his project. Not to be suspicious or anything, but mightn't there be a plot that they enjoin themselves to the task of cutting the island off, and then just let it float away?

By 1820 New York City was populated by 10,369 free Negroes, while 518 slaves were still registered within the city confines. Slavery in New York would not be abolished until July 4, 1827, but even after that there were gangs and individuals known as 'blackbirders' who would waylay hapless victims on the streets and back alleys to shanghai them for sale in Southern slave markets.

On Sundays and holidays, many Negroes would visit the city markets where they were joined by slaves from Long Island and New Jersey to partake in what was called 'Negro sayings and doings'.

They would carry with them everything they could muster, such as roots and berries, herbs, fish, clams, oysters, etc., in hopes of making a few pennies in pocket money.

Often they would be hired by some joking butcher or other individual to engage in a jig or breakdown known as 'Negro dancing', where they would show their skill by dancing on a shingle. The best of these dancers would carry their own shingle as part of their stock in trade. This board was usually five or six feet long and a few feet in width. The music, or time, was supplied by the dancer as he beat hands on the sides of his legs and the top of his heels.

The favorite dancing spot was at the Catharine Market at Cherry, Catharine, and Water Streets, where an area was reserved and cleared on the east side of the fish market in front of Burnel Brown's Ship Chandlery. Here the dancers, would compete for highest honors, that is, the most cheering and the most collected in the hat, and if money was not to be had, payment might be a bunch of eels or fish.

The most famous dancers, or 'shiners', of the day were a little wiry Negro slave named Ned, belonging to Martin Ryerson; Bobolink Bob, belonging to William Bennett; a fellow named Pinkster; and another known as Jack who was the property of Frederick De Voo, a farmer, described by John De Voe to his nephew Thomas, as a relative, although this De Voo spelled his name differently from the rest of the family. Frederick De Voo owned twenty acres of ground fronting on the other side of the East River, in what is now Williamsburg, Brooklyn.

As Uncle John remembered him, Jack was a smart and faithful man. He was brought up by, and was a long time with, Farmer De Voo, who thought a good deal of him.

Years later in his interviews with his nephew Thomas, Uncle John sadly remembered what happened to poor Jack, because after he had been set free by the law, he wound up becoming a 'loafer', and finally died in the market.

As De Voe told it, on the day Jack was made free, Farmer

De Voo, fitted his former slave out in a new suit of clothes from top to toe. He then turned to him and said, 'Jack, if you come home with me, you shall never want; but if you leave me now, my home shall never more know you.' But Jack could not be persuaded to return home to Brooklyn.

Soon Farmer DeVoo began hearing tales how Jack had fallen on hard times. Several butchers crossed the river and urged the farmer to take Jack back, but he staunchly refused, saying, 'The laws set him free and he left me – now let the laws take care of him.'

Racism, fear, and suspicion were never far from the collected white consciousness in the city, and there had been numerous vendettas and rumors and fits of paranoia directed against the city's Negro population, and would continue. As early as 1712, Negroes were reported to be heard crying, 'Goddamn all white people!'

The worst incident up until then, was the Great Negro Criminal Plot of 1741 where hundreds of Negroes were arrested, seventeen hanged, and thirteen burned at the stake.

Most recently a young Negro woman named Rose Butler had been convicted and sentenced to hang for setting her master's house on fire, with the intention of burning her mistress to death. She was convicted of arson by the verdict of a jury at the Oyer and Terminer, held on November 19, 1818, before Justice Thompson, and sentenced to die on June 11, 1819.

Her cause was taken up by Johnny Edwards, the 'scale-beam maker', an eccentric who was well-known for taking up on the east side of the Essex Market, before the hills were dug down. Here, on the average of once a week, he would entertain a large number of persons, orating from his favorite rock. After Rose Butler's conviction, Edwards began to focus all his energies on the young woman's cause, exhorting in the streets, markets, and churches, 'Blood for blood – but not for fire!'

On one occasion in a meeting house of the Baptist Church on Mulberry Street, Johnny arose and began exhorting the congregation until the sexton requested him to be quiet, as it disturbed the worshippers, to which Johnny reportedly answered, 'Glad on it – they ought to be disturbed.'

On the day of her scheduled execution hundreds upon hundreds turned up to see Rose's final demise, but the sheriff received a last-minute reprieve, the governor stating that one of the reasons for the ruling was the 'insanity' of the prisoner.

But the *Evening Post* claimed this postponement was merely an inducement to Butler, in the hope that she may make a disclosure of the name of some accomplices.

The paper charged, 'That she had accomplices is pretty certain though she denied it to one of the clergymen who attended her; for after she was confined in prison, the house was again set on fire, and burned to the ground; and we hear that threatening letters (of the rising of colored people) have lately been sent to the Mayor, if the execution should be carried into effect.'

On the day when the hanging finally took place, a large crowd of people assembled at the Bridewell, the prison in City Hall Park. 'From hence she was taken in a carriage to the Potters' Field in Washington Square. Mr. Bell, the Sheriff, performed his duty in person in his official full dress.

Rose made no disclosures of accomplices, and her last words were 'I am satisfied as to the justness of my fate – it is all right.'

A newspaper account in the *Columbian* of July 8–9 concluded, 'We are happy to learn that the colored people of this city, being convinced of the enormity of the crime, are generally reconciled to the fate of Rose Butler, and it is hoped that no offence of a similar nature will ever again occur.'

As bad as prospects and living conditions were for the Irish in the city, daily life could be worse for the Negroes. In the city's Fourth Ward, a large Negro ghetto spread from its heart on Bancker Street between City Hall and the East River, the area a blight of filth, dampness, overflowing privies, and contaminated drinking water.

The attitude of whites toward Negroes is exemplified by Charles Haswell in his memoir, *Reminiscences of a New York Octogenarian (1816–1860)*. In 1824 the height of fashion for women included chinchilla hats, blue shoes, and blue Canton crape dresses. To hear Dr. Haswell tell it:

I witnessed in great part the following scene. At this period and for many years after, until the street was sewered, all the surface water from the [City Hall] Park ran over a depression across Broadway, and down Vesey Street, and as a result, the gutter during a heavy rain or thaw would be kneedeep, involving the use of a board to bridge it. At this time the gutter was running very full from the effects of a thaw, and a man, well-dressed and of presentable appearance, had dragged a chinchilla hat from off the head of a negress, stamped on it, and then threw it into the gutter, where it was rapidly borne down the street. Upon being questioned why he had done it, he replied: 'I have just paid eighteen dollars for a chinchilla hat for my sister, and I don't mean that any niggerwench shall wear one like it, while I know it.'

Chapter Eight

In which Lozier takes it upon himself to draw up plans and blueprints for the special appliances needed to see the project through to its successful end, and begins to enlist blacksmiths and mechanics who will see the special tools made.

OVER THE NEXT FEW DAYS, Lozier stayed away from the market, leaving De Voe to handle the steady river of men still lining up to sign up for work – Jack Tars, Teagues (Irishmen), saucy boys, and bitter native-born Americans among them.

When asked where Lozier was, De Voe explained that he was in his workshop drawing up plans for the singular and very specific appliances needed to solidify the plans for sawing off the island.

Following some days absence, Lozier finally reappeared. He now had with him elaborate plans for the implements. The blueprints elaborated the giant saws that would be necessary to do the cutting proper. He showed the scale drawings to a select few of artisans, told how he had pored over them, making sure every indication was just as it should be. The prints called for whipsaws of a most singular nature, owing to their inordinate size, incredibly to be built one hundred feet in length with teeth extending to no less of a height of fully three feet above the body.

Fifty men, Lozier stated, would be needed to manipulate

each appliance. His conservative estimate called for at least twenty saws.

In addition, he said he had thought long and hard as to how to propel the island into the harbor once it had been successfully cut loose. He had carefully considered any number of alternatives, including the one of building massive iron stanchions to be positioned on the northern edge of Staten Island and in western Brooklyn, with their counterparts constructed along the lower East River, and at the tip of the Battery. Here he would secure specially woven hemp ropes of enormous length, tensile strength, and durability, and on the pulling end, position mighty teams of mules, horses, and oxen. These brawny beasts would act in concert to tear the sawn-off island loose from its moorings, while the ropes kept it on track.

But in the end, upon careful thought and final reflection, Lozier conceded, he had decided to abandon this tack.

The approach he had finally settled on, he now announced in deference to more than a few blacksmiths and ironmongers already in attendance at his invitation, would also call for a good deal of concerted ironwork. But instead of the gigantic stanchions and towers, the amended plan would call for only the vast cast-iron oarlocks to be constructed, each 'to be made in a peculiar but substantial manner'.

The plans necessitated twenty-four of these locks to be forged, twelve to be assembled along the East River at regular intervals from Corlears' Slip to Hellgate, twelve to be constructed on the Hudson at approximately the equivalent longitudes.

Each lock would be built to Lozier's carefully drawn

specifications in order to accommodate oars, or 'sweeps', as he called them, each 250 feet long, to be implemented on the opposite sides of the extreme flanks of Manhattan so as to sweep the severed island around after it was sawed off.

Lozier proudly announced the described plans called for posting fully one hundred men to each sweep.

The sweeps, of course, would themselves call for teams of highly skilled carpenters and joiners.

The idea was for the sawyers to get busy first thing. As soon as they finished their hacking work, and the island had come loose from its rootings, then the oarsmen would get to work, setting to on their prescribed monstrous, backbreaking task, eventually to use their powerful oars to propel the island down into the bay, before sweeping it around, given the clearance, and then bringing it back and reattaching it at King's Bridge.

There was a contingency plan. Should a storm arise while the men were working, with the titan force to carry Manhattan out to sea, long chains and heavy anchors would be used as insurance to keep the island securely tethered to the harbor bottom, lest it be swept away and lost forever.

The prescribed chains and anchors would likewise have to be jobbed out to capable blacksmiths, and bids would shortly be accepted in an orderly manner. Consideration on estimates would need to be submitted forthwith after the proper and necessary study.

The specifications for the ironwork was now handed over to a range of blacksmiths, carpenters, and mechanics, all hopeful their bid would be the one chosen so that they, too, could work on the immense project that would inevitably

bring all participants much glory with its successful completion, and they were eager one and all to partake in those
benefits such an undertaking would inevitably bring.

Each tradesman was requested to give full cost breakdowns
for labor, as well as fully elaborated estimates for materials
needed that would go into the manufacture of what Lozier
conceded were the most singular and unusual appliances.

A day later, an excellent blacksmith from the neighborhood of Centre Market approached Lozier and asked for his
ear in privacy. He said he had not been to market in some
weeks, but now had heard about the project and was very
anxious to partake in the work. He offered his qualifications.
On his own behalf, but with both modesty and humility, he
said there was no work in his line that he could not do.

He went on to tell Lozier that he had spoken with his wife
about the project, and although she had no faith in this job,
he had every faith, and he was presenting himself at this very
moment to receive the dimensions of each part of said
objects so that he might properly estimate on them.

Lozier carefully explained, giving no offense, that no man,
whatever his qualifications, would be favored over any other
man, if that's what the man was asking. According to Lozier,
this was the American way that all men were equal and
deserved to be treated equally.

The blacksmith said he understood, and desired no favoritism, only an equal chance to compete with his fellow
mechanics.

They shook hands, and, as an afterthought, Lozier men-
tioned that the blacksmith's skeptical wife was hereby
personally invited to apply for employment. Lozier told

the blacksmith how some of the other men were bringing their wives along to cook and clean and keep orderly camp, and the blacksmith's wife, if she was so doubtful, could come along and see for herself, all the while living in only the best accommodations and at the same time earning something more than a living wage.

Chapter Nine

In which Lozier has his first conversations with carpenters
and building tradesmen and makes preliminary overtures
to them.

LOZIER HAD ONCE BEEN well-connected in the building
trades. He had grown rich as a ship's carpenter and con-
tractor, and although presently retired, in some circles, he
still commanded respect.

He now began to seek out former associates, asking
recommendations, approaching contractors and carpenters,
grilling them about the feasibility of joining the endeavor,
and their ultimately supplying lumber and building housing
to shelter his workmen.

He asked for estimates of costs, specifying unequivocally
that a separate facility of the first order be contracted out for
the women who would accompany the men to King's Bridge,
coming along to cook, clean, and wash for the entire crew.
He pointed out that these women would be the wives of
some of the workmen, and needed to be treated as to their
proper station.

Their barracks, so Lozier made clear, must be built only
out of the best material in deference to the women's sex.

Lozier spoke of arrangements to secure a dozen loads of
lumber to be transported up to the banks of the Spuyten
Duyvil at King's Bridge.

Spuyten Duyvil is the name of the creek that separates

Manhattan Island from the Bronx. There is some speculation from where the name came. In all probability from the Dutch, Spuyten Duyvil referring to a spring that once 'spouted' from a hill near the northern end of the island and fed into the creek.

Some students of history say, however, that before the creek was widened and dredged to form a proper channel for ships, the tides of the Harlem and Hudson rivers would rush into the creek with such force that the resultant riptides would cause the water to literally spout into the air.

Variants of the name recorded through city lore include Spitting Devil, Spiking Devil, Spitten Devil, Spouting Devil, Spiken Devil, and In Spite of the Devil.

There is some talk that local Indians first called the creek 'Spouting Devil' because when Henry Hudson passed on his ship the *Half-Moon* on his way upriver for the first time, he fired his cannon at them, killing several innocent tribe members. From that time forward, the little stream was for good reason thus called, Spouting Devil, but as more than one historian notes, that presupposes that the Indians had some knowledge of English, and this before there were even any English afoot on the land, only Netherlanders.

In his whimsical *History of New York by Diedrich Knickerbocker*, Washington Irving tells his version of how the creek got its name. According to Irving, Antony Van Corlear was a trusted lieutenant of Peter Stuyvesant. When war loomed close with England for possession of New York, Stuyvesant sent out Van Corlear to warn those in the countryside to shoulder their weapons and march down to Manhattan to defend the city against the British armada.

'It was a dark and stormy night,' writes Irving, 'when the good Antony arrived at the creek which separates the island of Mannhata from the mainland. The wind was high, the elements were in an uproar . . . For a short time [Antony] vapored like an impatient ghost upon the brink, and then bethinking himself of the urgency of his errand took a hearty embrace of his stone bottle, swore most valorously that he would swim across in spite of the devil (Spyt den Duyvel!) and daringly plunged into the stream. Luckless Antony! scarce had he buffeted half-way over when he was observed to struggle violently, as if battling with the spirit of the waters – instinctively he put his trumpet to his mouth, and giving a vehement blast – sank forever to the bottom!'

Irving continues that there were 'witnesses' who swore they saw the 'duyvel' in the shape of a huge fish, a moss-bonker, seize the sturdy Van Corlear by the leg and drag him beneath the waves, and so said, the ghost of the ill-fated Dutchman still haunts the waters, and the adjoining promontory which projects into the Hudson and has been called Spyt de Duyvel, and so says the author, nobody attempts to swim across the creek after dark any more.

'On the contrary,' concludes Irving, 'a bridge has been built to guard against such melancholy accidents in future and as to the moss-bonkers, they are held in such abhorrence, that no true Dutchman will admit them to his table, who loves good fish and hates the devil.'

Over the next days, the contractors with whom he had spoken begged Lozier to give the word and they would gladly send work crews up to King's Bridge, and commence building the necessary barracks.

Lozier seemed to consider their suggestion, but in the end, put them off, saying without apology that he was not quite ready to act and must procrastinate, that he must first fully hire his crew, and set other forces in motion, before commencing on the construction of camp and quarters.

The hardened tradesmen were insistent nonetheless, itching to get to work on what amounted to such a huge project that would ultimately mean much money to them, but again, Lozier simply stayed away in order to avoid their insistence, returning a few days later, to be surrounded by the eager throng, but putting them off once more, telling them, with all due respect, he must for the time being reject their offer of starting up, reiterating once more that he first must settle the business of fully hiring his crew and arranging for their food and supplies over the long protracted length of the project.

When all this was satisfactorily completed, he would immediately set to, making sure all materials were properly gathered. Then and only then would he give the word for them to commence building.

This statement was met with great general disappointment. Some of the contractors adamantly voiced their opinion that Lozier's approach to the task at hand could only be a grievous mistake.

Lozier had informed them that once his crew was all assembled, he was planning to march the lot of them from downtown to up in a huge display of pomp and circumstance. It was his intention to assemble all his army of workers at some location downtown, yet to be decided, and amidst much glitter, and perhaps even fireworks, parade them up to King's Bridge attracting the most attention feasible to the project.

The contractors were abashed at such an ostentatious plan. Not so much as to the scope of it, but what will happen, they demanded to know, when Lozier's army arrives at the site of King's Bridge, ready to be put to work, and there is no place for them to stay?

Lozier cracked a crafty, knowing smile at such a notion.

He is well-prepared for the contingency, he tells them, because he has devised a revolutionary, never-before-seen plan of building that in one fell swoop will address all their concerns.

They begged him to reveal what this revolutionary plan could be. But he said he would not, under any circumstance, divulge its secrets until the time comes. But with this new construction method of his own invention, he assured them, all necessary building will be carried out and completed within only a few hours.

A few hours? This mysterious boast was met with a great deal of additional muttering and grumbling. Lozier's optimism seemed, at best, implausible.

Yet even the most vocal of the skeptics were quieted when Lozier reminded them that a good many of the frame houses of Greenwich Village had been thrown up virtually overnight, and under the most hectic and malevolent of circumstances after the recent yellow-fever epidemic had emptied the city, and had not a good many of the men, if not all, standing now in front of him been there to accomplish that work?

Chapter Ten

In which a vivid portrait of the city emptying in the face of yellow fever is given, and the consequences of the 'American Plague' on the poor, the principal sufferers, are cataloged.

WITHIN A WEEK, the heat of summer coming on, a different class of indigent people desperate for work began to find their way to Centre Market, to stand in front of De Voe and his ledger.

The hollow-eyed men took their places, breathed the fetid air shallowly, coughed fitfully into filthy handkerchiefs, looked suspiciously left and right at their fellows – equally hollow-eyed, equally shallow-breathed – waiting with them, and peered to the front of the line. How many more until it was their turn to sign in on the book?

Survivors. But barely.

Dreaded fever.

During the first quarter of the nineteenth century yellow-fever epidemics swept through New York City almost yearly to such an extent, the disease began to be known as the American Plague.

A viral infection afflicting the liver, acute and often fatal, yellow fever is carried by the *Aedes aegypti* mosquito.

But in the time of Lozier and De Voe's hoax, the source of the disease was unknown. Rather, transmission was believed to be caused by marshy polluted air containing the 'yellow fever miasma.' The miasma itself was thought to be an unknown, intangible 'effluvium' that crept into the air and infected all those with the bad fortune of living in its midst.

Once infected, be you rich or poor, one could be well in the morning and near death by night.

Fully, one-third to one-half of those contracting the 'implacable foe' expired in horrible circumstances.

Victims turned yellow and died in agony. Many of those suffering crawled into holes to breathe their last. Twisted out of shape, they were discovered later, only the terrible stench of rotting flesh giving a clue to where their bodies lay.

Symptoms included flushed face, dull pain, a red tongue, yellowing of the whites of the eyes and the skin of the body, nausea, black vomit like coffee grounds, convulsions, coma, and then death on the eighth day after initial contraction.

Some, mostly the well-off and gentry, blamed squalid conditions indigenous to the streets of the poorer and downtrodden neighborhoods: sunken yards filled with offal and scum, stagnant water, putrefying matter in ponds, open sewers, and overflowing privies.

'The disease is most fatal among those who live in filth and dirt,' observed Richard Varick, mayor of the city, early on in the century.

In response to the first outbreak of plague, the Board of Health would order strict quarantines and mass cleanups. Panic set in among the populace, and thousands, almost exclusively those financially able, would flee the city. Prosperous residents abandoned their homes with miraculous swiftness, thousands fleeing for upper Broadway, heading to the green fields of Haarlam Village, the Village of Green-wich, and across the river to New Jersey.

Quarantines kept ships out of port. Virtually all commerce halted. Merchants and their families fled, as did shopkeepers and businessmen.

Those remaining, the poor and marginally employed, fell victim to fever in ever increasing number, especially those living in low-lying neighborhoods, in the landfills, along the waterfront, in the shantytowns, and Bancker Street hovels east of City Hall Park.

Virtually the only place available to the poor for treatment was the New York Dispensary, established in 1790, and located on Centre Street at the corner of White.

Here, a sign over the door proclaimed:

I WAS SICK AND YE VISITED ME.

The dispensary was administered by nine attending physicians, an apothecary, an assistant, and six district physicians who traveled to those too feeble to leave their homes under their own power. There was no charge for treatment or medicine, as funds were sustained by corporate and state grants, private subscriptions, donations, and legacies.

Some sufferers were removed to 'pesthouses' by the Board of Health and Humane Society, while others filled the confines of the municipal buildings at Bellevue on the East River, especially set up to accommodate indigent fever victims.

Cookhouses were established to distribute soup, bread, and other meager sustenance.

In late spring 1822, the fever reappeared once again.

The first case broke out on June 17 on Rector Street, west

of Broadway, just below Trinity Church, in an upper-crust neighborhood, what had up until then been considered the healthiest part of the city. Because of the unusual circumstances of the occurrence, panic spread quickly.

By the middle of July, the epidemic had spread so decisively, the Common Council declared everything below City Hall an infected district. A picket-fence barricade was erected along Chambers Street. Quicklime and coal dust were spread in the streets, and fires were set all over the city in hopes of purifying the air.

By August, New York had taken on the appearance of a city besieged. The *Commercial Advertiser* reported, 'From daybreak till night one line of carts, containing boxes, merchandise and effects, were seen moving towards Greenwich Village and the upper parts of the city. Carriages and hacks, wagons and horsemen, were scouring the streets and filling the roads; persons with anxiety strongly marked on their countenances, and with hurried gait, were hustling through the streets. Temporary stores and offices were erecting, and even on the ensuing day (Sunday) carts were in motion, and the saw and hammer busily at work. Within a few days thereafter, the Custom-House, the Post-Office, the Banks, the Insurance Offices and the printers of newspapers located themselves in the village, or in the upper part of Broadway, where they were free from the impending danger; and these places almost instantaneously became the seat of the immense business usually carried on in the great metropolis.'

In the city proper, all business was soon suspended. The only souls remaining on the streets were weary doctors and gaunt men driving hearses.

Even daily ferry service from the wharves of Brooklyn to lower Manhattan now bypassed the tip of the island, proceeding north along the West Side to dock directly in the Village.

Virtually overnight, Greenwich Village became a boomtown.

At first, displaced people were sleeping in makeshift shelters out in the fields. Then wooden buildings sprang up almost instantaneously. One Saturday morning, reported the Reverend Mr. Marcellus, corn was growing in a field on Hammond Street (West Eleventh) and Fourth Street, and by Monday the field contained a structure capable of housing three hundred lodgers.

St. Luke's Church in the Field contracted with the carpenter James Wells to build a string of brick row houses, which the church immediately turned into rental properties.

Hudson Street was quickly lined with new homes aimed at the prosperous class, replete with new brass grates designed to burn anthracite coal, brick cisterns with pumps, and servants' quarters.

Smaller houses were erected to accommodate the flood of carpenters, painters, stonecutters, masons, and other artisans.

Christopher Street was quickly paved and flagstones laid for sidewalks.

The blocks around Newgate Prison, between Christopher and Amos (Tenth) Streets and situated on the river, were so in demand, plans were made to shut down the prison entirely and move the jailed upriver to a new facility, Sing-Sing, to be built in Ossining.

In the Village business was conducted out of temporary booths. Bank Street was named because banking offices, removed from Wall Street, were operating there. Even the post office moved here to the hinterlands.

Prices soared.

Talk began of abandoning lower Manhattan altogether and creating an entirely new city in Greenwich Village.

Although the epidemics of 1798, 1799, 1803, and 1805 had tended to solidify the villages, especially those around Spring Street and Newgate Prison, the epidemic of 1822 saw a marked change, a great many streets built up with a tidal wave of wooden buildings utilized for the most part by merchants and offices.

Meanwhile, medical thinking came to believe that these summers that were excessively sultry and excessively wet brought on the fever.

Dr. E. H. Smith theorized to his colleague Dr. W. Buel in a letter that got into the hands of Thomas De Voe that 'meats spoiled in the market place uncommonly quick, and those which were brought home, apparently fresh and good in the morning, were often found unfit to be eaten when cooked and brought to table later in the day. Esculent vegetables in general, and especially fruits, were usually poor, tough, and tasteless. The peach, particularly that of the clingstone, was scarcely digestible, and often occasioned temporary illness, quite severe, while it doubtless aided in the production or aggravation of the fever.'

Early on down in the city, all the occupants of the butcher stands and other stalls in Centre Market had been ordered to set up shop away from the infected areas, either in St. John's Park on Hudson Street or in Chatham Square.

But in truth few remained in the city and there were few for them to serve. Making matters worse, country people and local farmers were hesitant to enter the infected area with their provisions. The appointed fever committee, doing their utmost to provide some relief to the indigent and distressed sick, issued the following statement: 'We entreat our fellow citizens of the surrounding country not to withhold from the markets the usual supplies of poultry and small meats, as well as other articles so essentially necessary to both sick and well, in this city, in this distressed season.'

According to Uncle John, and reported by Thomas De Voe, sustenance was in such short supply, people were forced to forage in the most unlikely places, harvesting musk melons and green beans literally from the cracks of streets and sidewalks, 'the product of the seed thrown out by the inhabitants before they were driven thence by the pestilence, and which took root in the scanty soil between the paving-stones. What a striking evidence is this of the utter desertion of that part of the city by all human beings and domestic animals! And what a picture of desolation and germ does it exhibit!'

In their hovels those on the lower rungs of society continued to die in alarming number through the summer.

Grant Thorburn, in his memoir *Fifty Years' Reminiscences of New York; or, Flowers from the Garden of Laurie Todd* remembered vividly his toiling as a nailmaker one plague summer, recalling the children of the busy carpenter with whom he worked tramping through the streets hawking their wares, chanting, 'Coffins! Coffins for sale! Coffins of all sizes!' They offered the boxes for four dollars apiece.

Not until the weather of late October turned brisk, and November brought cold bone-chilling enough to kill the mosquitoes, did the human-death count subside.

Only then, with frost crackling on the ground, did the bankers and merchants begin to stream back to Gotham proper. Taking their cue, the post office returned to its old tenancy, and the countinghouses to Wall Street. The thrown-up residences of Greenwich Village were soon abandoned, as were any thoughts of moving the city.

As many, if not more, that had streamed out of the city, now streamed back in.

The dead were buried, hope was on the rise, the future was bright.

Quarantines were lifted. The riverside wharves again bristled with the many masts of commercial shipping. Penniless immigrants were once more streaming into the lower enclaves of Manhattan, looking for any work they could find.

Filth, grime, disease, poverty, overcrowding, confusion, and cacophony again permeated all but the most affluent streets.

The island was back to normal.

Winter came on, the weather so harsh the Hudson River froze solid from shore to shore; the brutality of the weather added more misery to the already suffering poor and destitute. The price of a load of oak wood for burning rose to five dollars a load, way out of the reach of those in need of warmth. Some butchers established soup houses in an attempt to keep the destitute fed, and collections were taken up in neighborhood churches for the benefit of those most in want.

As Philip Hone would soon observe in his diary: 'Irishmen and horses are plenty enough in New York, but means should be adopted to prevent such awful sacrifice of their lives.'

Pressed cheek to jowl, those hollow-eyed men waiting for Lozier and De Voe to put them to work smelled the sour scent of the man in front and the man behind, and when they turned their heads, they looked into the suspicious red-rimmed eyes of their fellows, so it was no leap for them to believe that the city was overburdened and the southern end ready to break off and sink into the harbor, and put every last one of them out of their misery.

Chapter Eleven

In which all the all the sawyer positions are filled and testing begins for those willing and able to 'go below'.

IT WAS ONLY A FEW DAYS later when Lozier stepped beside De Voe, ran a boney finger down the long, meticulously kept list of De Voe's green ledger book, and announced that all the sawyer positions were now filled.

There was a prolonged groan from the line of men still waiting for jobs in front of De Voe, but Lozier raised his hand to silence them.

He informed the disappointed that although he now had a sufficient number of sawyers for the work above ground, a good many pitmen were still needed, those long-winded enough to 'go below' to saw. These pitmen would have to prove prodigious lung capacity, because not only would they have to saw deep into the earth, but also beyond that depth into the brackish water.

For their skill they would be well-rewarded, receiving treble wages, but they could not be taken on their word as to their capabilities. They must undergo rigorous testing.

These tests would be scheduled soon. Right now, Lozier suggested that De Voe continue to take names in his ledger, and at a later date, he and his colleague would refer to the ledger and contact the candidates so that they might report to the market at a prescribed time for individual examination.

Few balked at the prospect of receiving such a generous stipend, triple the going rate of that of sawyer, which was already at a high standard.

Later in the day, over many beers and applejack, some animated discussion took place as to how would the examination proceed. Lozier was seriously tempted to test the men underwater, this being how they would have to toil, but it was pointed out to him that on the West Side a great deal of raw human waste was still being emptied into the river by the night-soil squad (mostly Negroes, attracted by the wages) in an attempt to keep the city's privies from overflowing and running into the street where the soil mixed with street muck and storm water in rank puddles. The filth in the river, which was often hindered from washing away by the confusion of pilings, piers, wharves, and docks, gave the area a terrible noxious odor, especially in the heat of summer.

It would be unfair to ask anyone to be tested in conditions such as these.

On the other hand, on the East Side, sharks were well-known to frequent the East River shore, especially those around the Catharine Slip, and perhaps there was a risk these predators would impede a true test for each man.

De Voe especially was of a mind to agree with this assessment. With some solemnity, he recounted the story of Sam Way to illustrate his concern.

Sam was a well-known character, an old fellow who worked at the Catharine Market. Sam's job was for the most part to keep the wooden floors and space around the market free of fish heads, scales, entrails, and other bits of fish that would be ground between the boards and in the joints of the cobblestones to fester beneath the feet of the fishmongers.

The fish sold in the market was brought in daily by boat and skiff from the Jersey shore and Long Island. The market stands sold both wholesale and retail.

But Sam had a sideline from his usual duties of the day. He was a well-known shark catcher, a fisherman of no small accomplishment.

The habit of the fishmongers was to throw any dead fish and entrails and all other fish waste into the waters around the slip. This garbage increasingly attracted a great many sharks. Hearing the cry 'Shirk around the slip!' Sam would drop his broom and mop and grab for his chain hook, baiting it as he hurriedly made his way to the slip.

It would be only a few minutes more that a new cry would go up: 'Sam's got one hooked!'

He was a remarkably strong man despite his age, and it would take some 'rassling', but no doubt Sam would soon lay the offending 'shirk' on the dock for all to see, and it was boasted for him, because he was a modest man, when he had taken as many as seven in one day, some of them as big as fourteen feet.

So in reflection, and being himself a fair man, Lozier concluded given the fact of the filthy water on the one hand, and Sam Way on the other, it might be unfair to be testing men in waters where their health and very lives could be put in jeopardy, and then again to troop over to the waterfront in the first place, whereas he and De Voe were already quite comfortable where they sat in Centre Market, so Lozier's decision was to test the men who would be pitmen right there in front of him in the market.

And that is what he announced he would do.

A few days later, he asked De Voe to refer to his list. Messages were sent out to all those who had signed up that they must report to the market at the prescribed date and time for their personal testing.

The testing went on for a full week in front of many gawking observers. The men were asked to hold their breath while miming the action of the whipsaw they would have to repeat, and repeat again. Lozier observed from his seat, and De Voe with his big pocket watch timed the length each could hold his breath while working in such manner, and duly recorded the results in his ledger – to be compared later on when all men had been tested, so that all judgments would be equitable, aboveboard, and without favoritism as to who would eventually mine this rich lode of jobs.

Chapter Twelve

In which the reader is offered a definition of the word *hoax*, and given a catalog of some early American practitioners.

DECEPTION AND CREDULITY, the need to deceive and the need to believe were the hand-in-hand co-conspirators in the hoax. If Lozier felt a pang of guilt, if De Voe himself felt remorse in any way for the string of poor wretches lolling in front of them Uncle John did not let on to his nephew.

The word *hoax*, according to the *Oxford English Dictionary*, is contracted from the word *hocus*, 'to fool or deceive'. *Hoax* first appeared in the English language shortly before the year 1800, meaning 'to deceive or take in by inducing to believe an amusing or mischievous fabrication or fiction; something erroneous told in such a manner as to impose on the credulity of the victim'.

Perhaps the first master of deception of any merit in the annals of America was none other than Benjamin Franklin, humorist, printer, inventor, the man who brought the electrical terms *battery*, *plus* and *minus*, *positive* and *negative* all into the lexicon via the results of his proverbial kite-flying.

Franklin started out as a printer. With publication of his *Poor Richard's Almanack*, he was not above telling an untruth to keep circulation robust, including predictions of natural disaster and imminent invasion by foreign armies. Still

Franklin found himself losing out to a competitor, Titan Leeds, publisher of *Leeds' Almanack*.

Leeds' publication concentrated heavily on astrology, and the public seemed to crave notions of the future predicated by the stars and moon. Taking note, Franklin predicted in *Poor Richard's* that Leeds would be dead within the year, even daring to prophesize the day and hour of his rival's imminent departure from this Earth.

When Leeds did not die, it did not stop Franklin.

In the next year's addition of his almanac, he published a second notice of Leeds' death, this time not noting it as a prediction, but listing it unequivocally as if it had indeed already happened.

The very much alive Leeds objected, but it did little good. The public insisted he was dead.

The facts that he lived and breathed, that his almanac continued to appear were considered the imposture. Leeds' circulation fell, while Franklin's rose dramatically, and the more Leeds protested, the better *Poor Richard's* did.

Year after year, Leeds' death was cited in *Poor Richard's*. Year after year Leeds refuted the report of his demise. Year after year the public denied he was still taking breath.

Finally, eight years later, Leeds passed away for real, and *Poor Richard's* took the opportunity to commend the man's friends and supporters for finally owning up to 'fact' of his death.

During the Revolution, Franklin again made effective use of calculated deception, this time to influence the outcome of the war.

The British were using German mercenaries called hessians to fight against the Continental army. Franklin published a letter he claimed had fallen into his hands and had it widely circulated. The broadsheet claimed a hessian count by the name of De Schaumbergh was receiving a special stipend for each of his soldiers killed during battle.

The letter from Schaumbergh to his battlefield commander Baron Huhendorf, stated that the count was upset because he wasn't being paid in a timely manner, and worse, that audacious British doctors were actually trying to save his injured men on the battlefield, and that accounting recorded hundreds too few dead, thus denying him funds rightfully his.

'You're robbing me by keeping them alive,' Schaumbergh was said to have railed.

Franklin had, in fact, written the letter, and as a result of his trickery, hessian field officers increasingly met with derision at the hands of their British counterparts, while disheartened hessian line soldiers deserted in ever-increasing numbers.

Franklin skillfully utilized yet another ruse to undertake the cause of the inequity he observed commonly exercised against women. He published the story of a Philadelphia woman by the name of Polly Baker. Miss Baker, Franklin wrote, had been arrested no less than five times for mothering five bastard children with five different men.

Franklin took up the woman's tale of woe, describing her fifth trial, vividly including her impassioned speech to the court.

When castigated by the judge for the poor job of mothering she was doing, Polly shot back that she could easily do a better job if the court wasn't having her arrested and tried at every turn.

And as for the fathers of the children themselves, she challenged, 'They have never been prosecuted even though they were as responsible, and made me false promises.'

Accounts of Polly Baker's trial and speech to the court were reprinted throughout the world, and in many ways it is acknowledged that Polly's alleged tribulations, as skillfully depicted by Franklin, became one of the first pointed and effective defenses for women's rights.

As her speech to the court concluded: 'I have hazarded the Loss of the Publick Esteem, and have frequently endured Publick Disgrace and Punishment; and therefore ought, in my humble Opinion, instead of a Whipping, to have a Statue erected to my Memory.'

It wasn't till later when no Polly could be accounted for that people realized she was a ruse, a hoax fabricated out of Franklin's imagination in order to use the press in advocacy for the rights of women.

Washington Irving was one who took his lessons well from Franklin.

Irving was a young writer who had already begun to make his mark on the world of letters and literature in the early years of the century. In 1807 Irving, his brother, William, and William's brother-in-law, James Kirke Paulding, began to pseudonymously publish a satirical journal of essays entitled *Salmagundi*, the name referring to a spicy hash made of minced meat, anchovies, pickled herring, and onions, served with oil and lemon juice.

In these pages, Irving first christened New York as Gotham, in the essay 'Chronicles of the Renowned and Ancient City of Gotham.' As the story went, in the thirteenth century unpopular King John wanted to buy a castle in the region of the village of Gotham, which meant 'goat town'. The local peasants, knowing what would be in store for them if he did, (John was by all accounts a ruthless murderer, a treacherous, lecherous, horrid man) set out to dissuade his majesty by any means necessary. The peasants pretended to be fools, working assiduously upon the good king's arrival to be seen raking the moon's reflection out of a pond, and later joining hands around a thornbush in a vain attempt to keep a stray cuckoo bird from flying away. Seeing the mad actions of the inhabitants, the king thought otherwise of taking up residency among such people, leaving the 'wise men' of the village gleefully laughing after his rapid departure: 'More fools pass through Gotham than remain in it.'

Irving later confessed in the afterglow of his success, 'One of the most tickling, dear, mischievous pleasures of this life is to laugh in one's sleeve – to sit snug in a corner unnoticed and unknown, and hear the wise men of Gotham, who are profound judges . . . pronounce from the style of our work, who are the authors.'

Less than two years later, on October 26, 1809, the following urgent notice appeared in the *Evening Post*:

DISTRESSING.

Left his lodgings some time since, and has not since been heard of, a small elderly gentleman, dressed in an old black coat and cocked hat, by the name of *Knickerbocker*. As there are some reasons for believing he is not entirely in his right mind, and as great anxiety is entertained about him, any information concerning him left either at the Columbian Hotel, Mulberry Street, or at the office of this paper, will be thankfully received.

P.S. Printers of newspapers would be aiding the cause of humanity in giving an insertion to the above.

Ten days later on November 6, a response appeared in the same paper as a letter to the editor, signed simply, 'A Traveler'.

To the Editor of the *Evening Post*:

Sir, – Having read in your paper of the 26th October last, a paragraph respecting an old gentleman by the name of *Knickerbocker*, who was missing from his lodgings; if it would be any relief to his friends, or furnish them with any clew to discover where he is, you may inform them that a person answering the description given, was seen by the passengers of the Albany stage, early in the morning, about four or five weeks since, resting himself by the side of the road, a little above King's Bridge. He had in his hand a small bundle tied in a red bandana handkerchief: he appeared to be traveling northward, and was very much fatigued and exhausted.

Another ten days passed before yet another letter appeared to the editor.

Sir, – You have been good enough to publish in your paper a paragraph about Mr. Diedrich Knickerbocker, who was missing so strangely some time since. Nothing satisfactory has been heard of the old gentleman since; but a *very curious kind of a written book* has been found in his room, in his own handwriting. Now I wish you to notice him, if he is still alive, that if he does not return and pay off his bill for boarding and lodging, I shall have to dispose of his book to satisfy me for the same.

I am, Sir, your humble servant,
SETH HANDASIDE

Landlord of the Independent Columbian Hotel, Mulberry Street

Twelve more days passed. Then on November 28, another curious announcement appeared in the paper.

LITERARY NOTICE

Inskeep & Bradford have in the press and will shortly publish,

A HISTORY OF NEW YORK

In two volumes, duodecimo. Price three dollars.

Containing an account of its discover and settlement, with its internal policies, manners, customs, wars, etc., etc., under the Dutch government, furnishing many curious and interesting particulars never before published, and which are gathered from various manuscript, and other authenticated sources, the whole being interspersed with philosophical speculations and moral precepts.

This work was found in the chamber of Mr. Diedrich Knickerbocker, the old gentleman whose sudden and mysterious disappearance has been noticed. It is published in order to discharge certain debts he has left behind.

On December 6, notice was finally given that the work had seen print:

A
HISTORY OF NEW YORK,
FROM
THE BEGINNING OF THE WORLD TO THE END OF THE DUTCH DYNASTY,
CONTAINING, AMONG MANY SURPRISING AND CURIOUS MATTERS, THE UNUTTERABLE PONDERINGS OF WALTER THE DOUBTER, THE DISASTROUS PROJECTS OF WILLIAM THE TESTY, AND THE CHIVALRIC ACHIEVEMENTS OF PETER THE HEADSTRONG – THE THREE DUTCH GOVERNORS OF NEW AMSTERDAM;
BEING THE ONLY AUTHENTIC HISTORY OF THE TIMES THAT EVER HATH BEEN, OR EVER WILL BE, PUBLISHED.
BY
DIEDRICH KNICKERBOCKER.

Knickerbocker, of course, was Irving. The advertisements and letters were a ploy that worked to perfection. *A History of New York* was an immediate success.

Decidedly with tongue in cheek, Irving skewered history in a hilarious blend of fact and fiction.

'According to the best authorities,' he begins, 'the world in which we dwell is a huge, opaque, reflecting, inanimate mass, floating in the vast ethereal ocean of infinite space.'

Much had been lost in regard to history of New York under the rule of the Dutch. The recently formed New York Historical Society had put out a cry for assistance, asking anyone with any knowledge of those days to please step forward and share all information at their disposal.

Irving it seems happily took up the gauntlet under the guise of his alter ego, Knickerbocker. *Knickerbocker* in Dutch literally means 'one with the habit of falling asleep over his reading matter,' and so Father Knickerbocker, as did the wise men of Gotham, became a symbol of the city that he had so well illuminated in his volume. As he writes in his preface, 'A city is nothing without its historian.'

An exercise in mythmaking, *A History of New York* is a hilarious bemoaning of present times pining for the good times of yesteryear.

Upon its premise, New York's early history was enjoyed and enjoined by the reader, accepted as fact, more or less, as a happy time of contented people, with little hardship or conflict or struggle to confront them.

No one really cared what was true or false. The flights of fancy led to serious historical delving. In the end, the end justified the means.

With publication and the book's astonishingly quick popularity, Irving gained a native audience and international reputation. An American literature was born.

Coleridge was said to have become 'rib-sick' from laughing. Dickens wore out his copy.

Virtually overnight, Gotham had roots, albeit questionable ones.

Chapter Thirteen

In which we learn about the project to build the Erie Canal, and why it had an impact on people believing in the reality of sawing off New York.

IN 1810, with the city still embracing Diedrich Knickerbocker's giddy confabulation of New York history, ex-mayor De Witt Clinton, a heavy-set man with clear hazel eyes and what was described as 'a complexion as pure as a woman's', threw in his lot with a group of land developers and economic visionaries who had been toying with the idea of digging a canal from the Great Lakes to the Hudson River.

Out of office after having served his city from 1803 to 1807 and again from 1808 to 1810, Clinton was appointed that summer by the New York State Legislature to the newly formed Board of Canal Commissioners.

Accompanied by a team of engineers and surveyors, he immediately undertook to travel up through the Mohawk Valley into the Finger Lakes and from there to the village of Buffalo, to ascertain a canal's feasibility.

The problems faced by such a massive undertaking seemed insurmountable. The distance to be transversed was immense. The Mohawk River Valley remained a wilderness, and the Montezuma Swamp a treacherous haven of fetid black water and mosquitoes. Not to mention, the oldest mountain chain in America, the Appalachians, stood in the way.

Clinton returned from the reconnaissance, estimating that the project would cost five million dollars.

Up until then, all commerce from the swiftly growing Great Lakes region and the interior of the continent, especially the Ohio River Valley, followed the great rivers to market, with goods floating down the St. Lawrence to Montreal, the Delaware to Philadelphia, and the Mississippi to New Orleans.

Although the Mohawk River in upstate New York did flow into the Hudson at the village of Rome, in order to reach this little river port from the west one had to travel overland at staggering expense. To transport wheat from the rural outpost of Buffalo to New York City, one had to pay three times the wheat's market value. For corn, the price was six times. For oats, twelve. Truth was, goods could reach the harbor of Montreal for one-third the expense it took to get to New York.

Because of this expense it was inevitable that New York was missing out to rival market centers. The city was no more than the fifth most important port on the continent.

After returning from his initial foray through the upstate wilderness, Clinton traveled to Washington to plead New York's case for federal support. He speechified that the building of the canal could transform the city and the entire Western world, at the same time hastening the taming of the frontier. All sorts of products from furs to flour, from lumber to anthracite coal, Clinton promised, would follow the confluence of waters to the metropolis.

President Madison remained unimpressed, rebutting that federal monies were not meant for projects of an 'internal 'nature', declaring that such usage of federal funds was in most likelihood unconstitutional, and at any rate the entire undertaking would probably cost more than the collected resources of the entire nation.

Only a few years before, President Jefferson had declared the project 'madness'. Now Madison saw no reason to change Jefferson's assessment. Detractors sneered, called the canal the 'Big Ditch' or 'Clinton's Folly'.

Undeterred, Clinton sought out other states interested in contributing funds for the project to their mutual benefit, exclusive of the federal government.

This course failed, however. Only Ohio was willing to come aboard and subscribe to the plan.

Returning once more to the New York State legislature with a proposal of a state-owned and -operated canal, Clinton finally won approval for his 'folly'.

But it was too late. War, what some were dubbing a second revolution, was again brewing with England, and seemed inevitable.

Finally, on June 18, 1812, war was declared by President Madison and the Congress of the United States of America on Great Britain.

New Yorkers were in two directions over the war issue. Although in the back alleys, near the waterfront, and in the boardinghouses of poor neighborhoods, there was no short-age of men who hated the British and welcomed war, among the more prosperous the thought of another prolonged conflict with the British was reviled. Despite England's policies on the high seas, certain in the merchant trade had made fortunes, but others, like the stranded sailors who had seen more than six thousand of their mates seized by British forces, cheered at the news, declaring at a huge mass meeting in City Hall Park that they were at the ready.

A resolution was drafted that all differences among citizens would be laid aside to concentrate on the war effort.

The shipyards, which had been dormant under the embargo, went back to work and within a few months, a new fleet of twenty-six privateers was ready for combat.

Early naval victories were bolstering, but prices soon began to rise, slowing business. As this came to pass, many New Yorkers changed their feelings toward the war and decided that commerce and profits were more important than country loyalty. Growing more and more frustrated, many manufacturers and merchants began ignoring restrictions altogether, and traded with the British forces in Canada. Some people were indeed getting rich, but the average man was beginning to starve and freeze as well. The city quickly found itself forced to distribute food and firewood to keep their citizenry alive.

During the summer of 1814, full panic set in. News reached New York that the British were not only threatening New Orleans, but had also succeeded in taking Washington and burning the Capitol building to the ground.

The newspapers proclaimed New York would be next.

Militia companies were hurriedly called up to protect the city.

Money and manpower again flowed into the war effort.

Newspapers, once critical of the war, cried out against the British, and American manufacturing, although in no way the equal to Europe, geared up once more.

Clinton who had lost a run at the presidency to Madison, on a no war, pro-commerce platform, changed his tune. Once again mayor, he now declared that he would rather die in a ditch than surrender his fair city.

But the war was never fought in Gotham, and the British never attacked. Their invasion army was defeated as they moved south on Lake Champlain from Canada, as were additional forces proceeding north through Maryland.

Within two weeks the anxiety over invasion and annihilation subsided.

Peace was agreed to on Christmas Eve in 1814.

Thanks to the war, New York's economy was again thriving. The waterfront was bustling. Ships couldn't be built fast enough. Working on the docks earned four dollars a day, be you a sailmaker, a caulker, or a rigger.

But the good times would be short-lived.

Prices began to fall almost immediately, and just kept on falling.

Hard times, so recently gone, were on their way back big time.

During the war and embargo, Americans had no choice but to rally around domestic industry. But as soon as peace was declared and the embargo lifted, Americans hungered for British manufacturing. British merchants loaded ship after ship with wares and sent them off to America, not even waiting for orders.

New York was flooded with foreign goods. Warehouses were full. And American buyers flocked to New York to feast on the feeding frenzy. Fleets of British cargo vessels were steaming into the harbor, quickly unloaded, the goods aboard heading for the auction houses.

British manufacturers were so eager to empty their stores, they were at first willing to sell at a loss. British produce, therefore, undersold American produce, and British manufactured goods undersold similar American manufactured goods. On the other side of the ledger, however, British ports remained closed to American shipping. American manufacturers and wholesalers began to suffer at the hands of the flood of British goods.

By late 1815 the damage was done. The American cotton and wool industries were staggering, and three-quarters of American factories had failed. At the same time immigrants were flowing into the city. The streets were dirty and stinking. Only Broadway, described by Thomas De Voe as the thoroughfare of fashion, taste, and beauty, was cleaned on a regular basis. All other streets were swept once a month, if that.

Rich shippers and merchants, concerned by what they saw on the streets and in the lower levels of society, blamed all public ills on drunkenness and the misappropriation of charitable funds to the poor.

The very people who had helped to orchestrate the crisis in the first place, getting rich off the sorry state of affairs, formed organizations like the New York Society for the Prevention of Pauperism in order to combat the problems that they saw, which they believed stemmed from sloth, drunkenness, and godlessness.

At the outbreak of war in the early summer of 1812, De Witt Clinton had tried to walk a tightrope between Federalist interests, those who had opposed the war in favor of commerce, and Republican interests, those who wanted the war effort coordinated and waged more efficiently. Later that year, he had run against his old nemesis, James Madison for the presidency of the United States, but was defeated 89 electoral votes to 131.

After his defeat, Clinton returned to the city mayoralty for the third time, remaining in office until 1815, when, stepping down from political office, he returned to his vision of the Erie Canal.

Following peace, thousands began emigrating west, establishing farms and shipping their bounty east overland to Baltimore via the newly cut National Road, which extended from Indianapolis through Columbus to Wheeling, West Virginia, on to Philadelphia, now linked to Pittsburgh by turnpike.

As 1815 drew to a close, Clinton met with a group of businessmen at the City Hotel, urging them to provide support for the Erie Canal, assuring them that with its successful completion, New York would become the 'greatest commercial emporium in the world'.

He told the businessmen that he foresaw a city that would one day extend from one end of the island to the other, from the Battery to its northernmost tip at King's Bridge.

When he spoke like this in 1810, listeners scoffed and hissed at him. Now suddenly people recognized the possibility.

Clinton wanted construction to begin immediately, but he still had stalwart opponents who took glee in denigrating the project as his 'big ditch', grumbling that the whole fiasco was a transparent vehicle for his political ambition.

Clinton proposed again taking the plan to Washington for federal aid, but here, too, he was stymied. Nothing had changed in the nation's capital. President Madison wanted nothing to do with the project, still arguing the federal government had no place in financing 'internal improvements' for any individual state.

Back in New York, bitter with what he saw as Madison's undisguised efforts to keep New York from ascending, Clinton urged the state to assume responsibility unto itself.

In early spring of 1817, New York finally authorized the plan, and in June, riding the excitement, Clinton was elected governor in an overwhelming landslide. On July 4, three days after Clinton took office, the project to begin building the Erie Canal formally began, totally financed and owned by the State of New York.

The project presented problems of immense and unheard-of difficulty. Not only did the 'river need to be carved through the mountains', it needed to stretch forty feet wide, four feet deep for 363 miles. It would need 18 aqueducts and 83 stone locks in order to rise and descend an overall distance of 660 feet over its course, following the Mohawk and Niagara Rivers and the Torernanta and Tonnawanda Creeks through Syracuse, Rochester, and Utica.

The Erie Canal was America's first huge engineering project. It was remarked that those who worked on it attended America's first school of engineering, the men who ran the project having no formal training in the field, learning on their feet as the project progressed, acquiring the skills to survey and plan, and when necessity dictated, inventing machinery and tools, including a grubbing machine capable of tearing the stumps of forty trees out of the ground in a day and a new, hydraulic cement able to harden quickly underwater.

But more than anything, the project needed a huge supply of able-bodied manpower, and that was provided in a good part by 'Irish backs,' desperate immigrants who were streaming into the country from Ireland.

Mostly farmers and laborers from the Irish countryside they were looked down upon and loathed by most New Yorkers. Local citizenry made their feelings known toward these 'bogbusters' by fashioning effigies of them out of cast-off clothing and rags. Molasses was smeared on the slash mouths, potatoes and codfish strung around the necks, a whiskey bottle stuck in one pocket, and the stuffed dummies paraded through the street or hung from a tree or lamppost.

The canal workers labored under appalling circumstances, digging from one red-painted wooden survey stick to another, through rock and mud and thick woods, scared to let up because ten men stood in the wings ready to take their jobs.

Over the course of one summer while working in the Montezuma Swamp south of Syracuse, more than a thousand workers were struck down by typhus and malaria.

Most died.

The pay was ten dollars a month, plus plenty of drink. Barrels of whiskey were placed all along the line as encouragement to workers.

When the project was eventually finished in 1825, two years ahead of schedule, it was a feat of engineering marvel, human ingenuity, and human toil on a scale America had never known.

With its much-talked-about and anticipated completion near, anything seemed possible.

Sawing Manhattan in half?

Lozier and De Voe sat back, feet up, gazing placidly at the line of prospective poor souls in front of them.

A piece of cake!

Chapter Fourteen

In which Lozier deems it time to approach butchers so that there will be an ample supply of meat for his workers, and two among their rank undertake a plan to outflank their butchering brethren.

THE BUTCHERS IN THE MARKET stood on the sideline over the course of all the hiring and talk of sawing New York off, for the most part keeping out of it, holding their tongues.

Then some of the men, in their long white aprons and top hats, started coming around, taking time out from their daily chores, not saying much, but hanging closer, clearly interested in what was going on. If this sawing business was a good thing, if there was business to be done and money to be made, there were those in their ranks who did not want to see it pass without counting them into this particular equation of commerce.

When Lozier noticed the interest of some of the butchers, he dispatched De Voe into their ranks, since De Voe, by being a retired butcher, was held by some of the fraternity in high esteem in his own right.

He went to them one at a time or a few at a time, and in confidence told them the sawing-off project would immediately need prodigious resources in order to keep the work crew properly fed to the high standard Lozier prescribed. And once in place, a steady flow of meat would be needed to keep the men going through the inevitable turmoil necessary to achieve their goal.

To begin, he and Lozier would be placing an order for some five hundred head of fat-beef cattle, five hundred pigs, and three thousand chickens.

Not surprisingly, the butchers' eyes widened.

The chickens were especially important, De Voe told them, because Lozier had generously promised his workmen chicken dinners served twice weekly, on Thursdays and Sundays.

The butchers considered what such an order would mean, and their excitement grew accordingly. Word spread not only through Centre Market, but through neighboring markets as well. Hearing the news, even the most skeptical butcher among them did not want to take the chance to be left out, and became greedy with the prospects.

Prices in the market rose quickly.

Two Centre Market butcher brothers, Stephen and John Hilliker, Stephen from Stall No. 7, John of Stall No. 4, in hopes of beating out the competition, undertook to buy fifty hogs, and once assembled drove them north along the Bloomingdale Road to King's Bridge.

Upon arrival they built pens so that the pigs would be there for the work crews when they arrived. It entailed an expense, but the brothers felt the gamble calculated and worth it.

The hogs remained at King's Bridge for a month with no word from Lozier or De Voe, nor sign of the imminent arrival of the work crew.

The Hillikers could only watch and stew as their hogs grew skinnier day by day in their pens.

Chapter Fifteen

In which we get a discussion of the newspapers of the day and their failure to cover the story of sawing Manhattan in half, but how a few years later, penny papers became a hotbed for hoaxes and humbugs.

IN THE COMING WEEKS and months, all through the course of Lozier and De Voe's scheme, there was never a discoverable mention of their plans to saw Manhattan in two in the press.

As explanation, that very well might have been because the established press of the time was aimed at a privileged readership, with little or no interest in the travails of the common working man. By the same token, the conventional political and mercantile fare that made up the daily news of the expensive subscription bulletins was of little interest to your everyday bloke or b'hoyo.

Herbert Asbury offers explanation for what otherwise would seem inexplicable. By his account in *All Around the Town*, 'Sawing Manhattan Island off soon became the principal subject of argument and conversation at Centre Market, and elsewhere as news of the great project spread. Neither then nor later, however, did the few newspapers of the period pay any attention to Lozier's activities. It is doubtful if the editors ever heard of him, for in those days the only way of transmitting intelligence was by word of mouth, or by letter, which was even more uncertain. Important happenings in one part of the city did not become generally known for weeks or months, and frequently not at all.'

In 1820 the two largest newspapers in the city, each with a circulation of two thousand, were the *Commercial Advertiser*, edited by Colonel William Lester Stone, and the *Evening Post*, edited by William Coleman. Four years later the daily publication of newspapers in New York had risen to fourteen thousand, although editorial focus had not changed.

'The *Advocate*, a leading paper, both political and social, had three thousand subscribers,' Charles Haswell tells us in *Reminiscences of New York by an Octogenarian (1816–1860)*, using their available 1823 column space to complain that 'a young man had been seen smoking in the streets so early as nine o'clock in the morning'.

The first page of the *Commercial Advertiser* was generally used to hawk goods and services, including such items as window blinds, Greek New Year cakes, anthracite coal from Pennsylvania, and Dr. Dyott's Approved Anti-Bilious Pills, which were touted as 'preventive and cure for all bilious complaints and malignant fevers'.

The paper's articles tended, as Asbury charges, not to focus on the city at all, but to engender a higher tone, even international in interest.

For example on July 2, 1824, the *Advertiser*'s readers were offered this scintillating news:

A steamboat purchased for the King of Denmark, and most splendidly decorated and furnished, has sailed from England for Copenhagen in which his majesty and family are to embark to visit Jutland and other places in the course of the summer.

Or, as on the fourteenth of that month, an editor at the *Advertiser* sullenly lamented in print:

Lord Byron. The separation of the great poet from his wife, not long after their marriage has ever been viewed with more interest, and a deeper feeling of regret, than any domestic occurrence of the kind of which we have ever heard.

In a time of humbugs it was the press, its widespread appeal and air of authority, that lent a hoax its true forum and power.

Before penny papers, newspapers like the *Commercial Advertiser* and the *Evening Post* were expensive, six cents an issue, and they weren't even sold on the street. They contained mostly shipping news and were mailed by subscription. What passed for news was communicated by semaphore from Sandy Hook to Staten Island to the Battery, announcing the imminent arrival of packet ships from England.

But things were about to change, and speed of reporting would soon be everything, accommodated by swift trains, boats, and horse express. By 1830 New York would boast forty seven newspapers, eleven of them dailies, and in 1833 Horatio David Sheppard began the *New York Morning Post*, under the editorship of Horace Greeley. Selling for two cents a copy, the paper was unsuccessful. Nine months later, a printer by the name of Benjamin Day got the idea to give the public more of what they wanted. He started the *New York*

Sun, selling it for only a penny a copy, and concentrating on the news he thought the public wanted: lurid reports of crime and scandal.

Within four months of its start-up date, the *Sun* had established itself as the most widely read newspaper in New York.

The paper concentrated on local crime and sports; colorful coverage of sensational murder trials led to its denunciation as nothing but a gutter press. Editorial attacks led to libel suits.

Philip Hone griped that the penny papers aimed at the 'most vitiated appetites' of their readers, featuring 'nauseous doses of personal slander, in which scandal is retailed to all who delight in it at that moderate price, disturbing the peace of the living and raking amongst the ashes of the dead'.

Newsboys, 'gangs of troublesome boys', as diarist and one-time mayor Hone put it, hawked the papers with the latest local, national, and international news on street corners, boosting circulation.

Some years later, Dickens would lampoon the practice in his commercially failed novel of America, *Martin Chuzzlewit*.

As his hero, Martin, reaches New York Harbor in steerage aboard a packet boat, the pushy newsboys swarm aboard, hawking their wares:

> 'Here's this morning's New York Sewer!' cried one. 'Here's this morning's New York Stabber! Here's the New York Family Spy! Here's the New York Private Listener! Here's the New York Peeper! Here's the New York Plunderer! Here's the New York Rowdy Journal! Here's all the New York papers!' . . .

'Here's the Sewer!' cried another. 'Here's the New York Sewer! Here's the Sewer with the best accounts of the markets and all the shipping news, and four whole columns of country correspondence, and a full account of the ball at Mrs. White's last night, where all the beauty and fashion of New York was assembled; with the Sewer's own particulars of the private lives of all the ladies that was there! Here's the Sewer! Here's the Sewer's exposure of the Wall Street Gang, and the Sewer's exclusive account of a flagrant act of dishonesty committed by the Secretary of State when he was eight years old; now communicated at a great expense, by his own nurse. Here's the Sewer! Here's the New York Sewer! Here's the wide-awake Sewer; always on the look-out; the leading journal of the United States. Here's the Sewer!'

The penny papers were immediately successful. People tended to believe what they read, and once the cheap newspapers gained hold on people, hoaxes of a grand scale proliferated and became well-documented.

In the case of the *Sun*, within two years, circulation had crept up to fifteen thousand, an unheard-of level then. But given its low price, the paper needed still more readers to be truly profitable.

A young assistant editor, Richard Adams Locke, was given the task of doing something to generate *Sun* readership.

Locke had recently taken note of an announcement that the famous English astronomer Sir John Herschel was setting sail for South Africa to study the galaxy from a different perspective than heretofore had been observed.

Locke, English by birth and education, came up with a scheme he was sure would pique public interest and boost sales of the *Sun*, so he presented the plan to his boss.

On August 21, 1835, a small report, supposedly emanating out of Edinburgh, Scotland, appeared on the front page of the newspaper.

'We have just learnt,' the notice began, 'from an eminent publisher in this city that Sir John Herschel, at the Cape of Good Hope, has made some astronomical discoveries of the most wonderful description, by means of an immense telescope.'

The article went on to describe the lens of the telescope as a vast forty-two feet across. The instrument in its entirety weighed a staggering seven tons and could magnify objects 42,000 times so that every little detail of the moonscape could be seen clearly.

Herschel was said to have spotted living creatures frolicking amidst lakes and forests on the surface of the moon. It was hard to describe the creatures as wholly human, because they were more like spotted pelicans or giant bats, although the creatures as observed did exhibit some distinctly human characteristics and behavior, spending 'their happy hours eating, flying, bathing, and loitering about'.

As viewed through the giant lens, they appeared to be about four feet high. They were yellow in color with wings made from a thin membrane. The wings, extending from the top of their shoulders to the calves of their legs, were without hair, and lay snugly upon their backs when not busy flapping.

The story caused an immediate sensation and made the *Sun* the best-selling daily newspaper in the country overnight, its circulation jumping to nineteen thousand. A special pamphlet edition, incorporating the six-part series in its entirety, sold out its sixty-thousand-copy print run.

Finally, after ten days of breathless craziness, the *Journal of Commerce* exposed the hoax, revealing the original idea to have been that of Locke.

Interestingly enough, most readers weren't upset and didn't voice any displeasure. Locke even went on to publish a book entitled *The Moon Hoax, or A Discovery that the Moon Has a Vast Population of Human Beings* that continued to sell extremely well over an extended period of twenty years.

One of those especially influenced by Locke's outlandish flimflam was Edgar A. Poe. At the time of the *Sun* moon hoax, Poe was working on a moon-hoax story of his own. His involved a hot-air balloon and was tentatively entitled 'Voyage to the Moon' after a similar story a professor of his, George Tucker, had been writing while Poe attended University of Virginia.

Beaten to the punch by Locke, Poe changed his idea somewhat, and it became instead his story, 'The Adventures of Hans Pfall', replete with an afterword making a case why Poe was not fooled for a minute by Mr. Locke's hoax, especially the mathematics which were ludicrous when the numbers were analyzed.

Still Poe had become enthralled by the machinations of the *Sun* moon hoax and kept the extraordinary impact of the incident in his mind.

A few years later, Poe had married his thirteen-year-old cousin, Virginia Clemm. Her mother, his Aunt Muddie, also lived with the couple. Poe was desperate for money to help finance his little family's move to New York from Philadelphia. He went to the *New York Sun*, the very newspaper that had done so well with the moon hoax, and presented an idea of his own.

A few days later on April 12, a special notice appeared in the form of a bulletin on the front page of the paper:

Atlantic Ocean Crossed by Balloon.
ASTOUNDING
NEWS!
BY EXPRESS VIA NORFOLK!
THE
ATLANTIC CROSSED
in
THREE DAYS!

———

Signal Triumph
of
Mr. Monck Mason's
FLYING
MACHINE!!!!
Arrival at Sullivan's Island
near Charleston, S.C.
of Mr. Mason, Mr. Robert
Holland, Mr. Henson, Mr.
Harrison Ainsworth, and
four others, in the Steering
Balloon 'Victoria'
After a passage of
Seventy-Five hours
From Land to land

After this teaser, which purportedly reached the *Sun*'s offices thanks to a SPECIAL DISPATCH VIA RIDER FROM THE SOUTH, the *Sun* promised to run a full extra edition the following morning.

When the paper finally appeared the next morning, huge crowds awaited, and all copies were quickly snatched up.

As promised, the story told the tale of two known aeronaut daredevils, Thomas Monck Mason and Robert Holland, both of whom were real enough, having already managed a long-distance flight from England to Germany via balloon.

According to Poe's unsigned account, the two, accompanied by six other aviators, had set out to cross the English Channel on their way to Paris, when a screw on the innovative rudder construction had come undone and they were caught up in a huge wind stream. Their course was altered remarkably in the opposite direction, and they had been blown clear across the Atlantic to set down on the coast of South Carolina, rather than the Champs-Elysées.

The newspaper account included not only a meticulously fact-based reportage, but also a vivid day-by-day journal. The story was never doubted until authorities in South Carolina went to the site and found no trace of the voyagers. The *Sun* admitted only that they had not as yet received confirmation of the story.

The incident was eventually revealed as a hoax created by Poe. Using his penchant for imaginative realism and his love of science and mathematics, he had constructed what seemed entirely fantastic, but plausible. Evidently, Poe surmised, people will believe exactly what they want to believe.

And so it was for Lozier and De Voe.

By De Voe's admission they had no idea their little joke would go on so far, but when it did, they had no other choice but to follow what they had started to its end.

Chapter Sixteen

In which we are further introduced to the king of the hoax
and learn about some of the humbugs he perpetrated.

IN THE EARLY 1830S, some six or seven years after Lozier and
De Voe orchestrated their alledged humbug Phineas T.
Barnum arrived in New York. He was running a boardinghouse with an attached grocery store in lower Manhattan,
not making a real good go of either of them, when he heard
from a friend of a curiosity on sale in Philadelphia.

Joice Heth was an 161-year-old slave, presently being
exhibited as a curiosity to the public. Her owner claimed she
had been born in 1674, and had been nurse to George
Washington from the time of his birth. She was said to have
been bought by Washington's father, Augustine Washington, and had been, in her words, 'the first person to put
clothes on the unconscious infant' and had 'raised' him. An
aged bill of sale, dated February 5, 1727, describing Heth as
being fifty four years old then, was in the possession of the
current owner.

Barnum went immediately to the City of Brotherly Love,
bargained the asking price down from three thousand dollars
to one thousand, and within a few months had Heth in New
York and on display.

Using an interlocutor by the name of Levi Lyman to draw
her out in front of the public, Barnum set Heth on stage in a
high divan in the center of the exhibition room where she

was made to feel comfortable enough by Lyman to answer questions, sing hymns, and tell stories about 'dear little George, Father of our Country'.

Using handbills, posters, and two backlit transparencies to bring in the crowds, who flocked in in such numbers that they could not be held back, Barnum very quickly was bringing in fifteen hundred dollars a week, drawing tens of thousands of curiosity seekers to view for themselves the 'Greatest Natural and National Curiosity in the World.'

The penny papers couldn't get enough of Heth and further fueled the public's interest by describing her as a 'renowned relic' and 'an Egyptian mummy just escaped from the Sarcophagus'.

But when ticket sales began to slack off as they inevitably must, Barnum had another brilliant idea to keep things going properly.

He wrote a letter to the newspaper, signing himself, vaguely, as 'A Visitor'. In the missive he charged that Joice Heth was a fake and a humbug. Not only wasn't she for real as the nursemaid of George Washington, she wasn't even human. She was a clever automaton, 'made up of whalebone, India-rubber, and numberless springs', given voice by the exhibitor, Lyman, who was a ventriloquist.

This astonishing revelation brought the crowds back with renewed fury. In droves they lined up, eager to ascertain for themselves whether Joice Heth was human or not.

It was here with his first hoax, that Barnum learned that people did not care if they were being fooled, as long as they enjoyed themselves and were entertained. As long as the public had something to talk about, they would pay, even to be humbugged. What was real and what was not did not matter.

Heth, too, was said to be enjoying herself, taking great delight in her newfound celebrity. Unfortunately, she soon fell ill, and by midwinter she was dead. Her corpse was carried back to New York City by sled from the home of Barnum's brother in upstate New York, where she had been cared for while infirm.

In the midst of great hoopla, arrangements were soon made by Barnum to cash in one final time. He announced the truth was going to be ascertained about the ancient slave once and for all. A surgeon was engaged. His job would be to perform a public autopsy in front of a huge audience.

Richard Adams Locke had ascended to the position of editor of the *Sun* on the strength of his moon hoax. He made sure to secure a seat front row–center for the spectacle.

At the end of the postmortem, the physician made his announcement. In no way was Joice Heth as old as she said. Instead of 161, the doctor said, clearing his throat, he put her age at eighty at the most.

The following day the *New York Sun*'s headline blared, 'Dissection of Joice Heth – Precious Humbug Exposed!'

On the day after that, Levi Lyman paid a visit to the offices of the *New York Herald*, personally calling on James Gordon Bennett, the editor/publisher.

Bennett himself was held in some renown for his sensational ways, and had engendered more than some bitter feelings.

Another New York journalist and editor, the future poet Walt Whitman, loathed Bennett, describing him as 'a reptile marking his path with slime wherever he goes, and breathing mildew at everything fresh and fragrant; a midnight ghoul, preying on rottenness and repulsive filth; a creature, hated by his nearest intimates, and bearing the consciousness thereof upon his distorted features, and upon his despicable soul; one whom good men avoid as a blot to his nature – whom all despise, and whom no one blesses.'

Lyman sat down in the 'reptile' Bennett's office and began telling him an astonishing tale. Not only was Joice Heth not really dead, but she was, at this very moment, performing in Connecticut. The autopsy had been undertaken on an old Harlem 'Negress' who had recently passed away.

Bennett was delighted. He especially took pleasure in the fact that his chief competitor, Locke, had been duped. He furiously took notes and a few days later the *Herald* printed the revelation as Lyman had told him.

Bennett, of course, was fit to be tied when he learned the truth, but remarkably the Joice Heth affair did not end there. Lyman came back, hat in hand, begging Bennett's forgiveness. Barnum made him do it, he wept.

Now he tearfully offered Bennett the true story of Joice Heth, how she was discovered in a Kentucky outhouse, how her teeth were extracted to make her look older, how she was taught the story of George Washington while her fake bill of sale was carefully being aged in tobacco juice.

Once again, Bennett fell for Barnum's ploy, just as Barnum knew he would. In four long articles, Bennett printed exactly what Lyman had told him, declaring, finally here was 'the absolutely real and true exclusive' account of Joice Heth. Unfortunately, to Bennett's chagrin, yet again it all proved made up.

Barnum was not finished with Lyman. He was to appear again in another of the great showman's crazy hoaxes.

Barnum had heard stories of an embalmed mermaid who had fallen into the hands of a Boston sea captain in Calcutta.

Barnum contacted the present owner, who traveled to New York bringing the mermaid with him in a long, polished oblong box.

Calling upon Barnum in his lower Broadway offices, the man unveiled the creature, and what Barnum saw both startled and impressed him. Lying in the box was a large fish body and tail expertly sewn onto the torso (replete with ponderous breasts), shoulders, and arms of a female orangutan. The head was that of a baboon.

Barnum immediately saw moneymaking possibilities in the creature, but only if his name was in no way associated with it. The debacle following the death of Joice Heth was fresh in the public's memory.

Instead, he assigned the 'mermaid' to the proprietorship of Dr. J. Griffin, an English naturalist-in-residence on leave in New York from his prestigious post at the Lyceum of Natural History in London.

Griffin, in actuality was Levi Lyman, made over to look altogether different in a new set of clothes, and sporting a British accent.

Barnum made arrangements to have ten thousand pamphlets printed, along with an eight-foot-tall color transparency to be hung outside the New York Concert Hall on Broadway, showing a fetchingly beautiful, bare-breasted creature rising out of glistening waters.

'Mermaid Fever' seized the city. On opening night thousands streamed into the concert hall, including many prominent naturalists.

What they got was 'an ugly, dried up, black-looking thing covered with black stringy hair'.

Even Barnum admitted it was something that 'looked like it had died in great agony'.

Still, once again, even with the knowledge that they were being humbugged, the crowds thronged to see.

It was Barnum's most lucrative exhibition yet. The 'Critter', as he called her, the incredible 'Fejee Mermaid', Barnum's 'Mysterious Lady Fish', drew profits of one thousand dollars a week during her New York stay.

The inevitable culmination of the Barnum hoaxes was a perfectly executed hoax of a hoax. This humbug occured a few years after Thomas De Voe's *Market Book* had been published, and involved a purportedly fossilized man who was to become known as the Cardiff Giant.

In the late 1860s George Hull was a cigar manufacturer living in Binghamton, New York. One summer he undertook a trip to Iowa to visit his sister and her family. She was very religious, and one day took him to a holy-roller, fire-and-brimstone prayer meeting run by an evangelist called the Reverend Turk.

The Reverend Turk, citing the book of Genesis, sermonized about a time on Earth when the land was populated by giants.

This got Hull thinking.

He found a quarry near Fort Dodge and traded a barrel of beer for a massive slab of gypsum, twelve feet long, four feet wide, and two feet thick. The gigantic block of hard stone weighed ten thousand pounds.

Hull loaded it up with the idea of shipping it by railroad to Chicago, but on his way to the rail yard some forty miles away, the heavy load broke down several wagons and a few bridges.

Finally Hull got the slab to Chicago where he hired an artist and a stonecutter, with the understanding they were to make him 'a naked giant'. He told the pair he needed the result to be anatomically correct in proportion to its size, and he wanted the figure to look 'like he died in great agony'.

Four months later, Hull had himself a stone man ten feet, four and half inches in height, weighing 2,990 pounds. The figure was skewered slightly to the right, its left foot drawn up and contorted, the right arm strewn across the abdomen, the left, folded up under the back.

Skin pores had been suggested by walloping the sculpture with a special mallet outfitted on its hammering surface with darning needles. The stone was aged in a diluted sulfuric-acid bath, and the natural veins in the gypsum appeared as if they were blood vessels.

Hull paid off the stonecutter and sculptor and swore them to secrecy. In a crate stenciled with the single word MACHINERY, he shipped his creation back home where he enlisted his cousin Stubby Newell, a farmer who lived thirteen miles south of Syracuse in the village of Cardiff, New York.

In the dead of night, Hull and Newell dug a grave, and buried the giant three feet deep in the soil. Then they covered him up and reseeded the ground.

Hull instructed Cousin Stubby not to touch this area of ground for at least a year.

As luck would have it, not long after the stone man had been buried, on a piece of ground not a mile away in Cortland, New York, a farmer, who had been plowing his field came across a pile of bones. The farmer called in scientists from nearby Cornell University in Ithaca, and the bones were ascertained to be genuine fossils.

Meanwhile, Hull had coached Newell to complain to his friends and neighbors that his well was drying up and that he was looking for someone to drill him a new one.

On some local recommendations, Stubby hired a crew, and using a dowser's wand in front of them, meticulously searched his property from one end to the other for a likely place to dig a new well. He finally settled on an area and instructed his diggers to put their backs to it while he went into town in hopes of securing a loan from the local bank in order to see the project through to completion.

Returning later that afternoon, having had no luck in the finance department, Stubby found a small crowd gathered behind his house.

Feigning alarm, he rushed into their midst, worrying loudly if one of the well diggers had been hurt.

He was assured no, no one had been hurt; instead his attention was directed to the open grave.

In a breathless tone, the chief well digger began to explain what had happened. Apparently the workmen had begun their task, but hardly had gone down three feet, when they uncovered part of a human body. Alarmed, they carefully uncovered the rest. Seeing what they had, they went running, and everyone who had got wind of what had been discovered was now here. Word was spreading like wildfire, so much so that Stubby Newell hurried into town and bought himself a big white tent, which he soon set up over the open grave. By the next day, enterprising Stubby had set himself up a ticket booth, too, and begun charging fifty cents a head for the privilege to peer at the giant.

Excitement spread. Four preachers showed up and pronounced the man in the grave irrefutably human, dating him back to biblical days just as Preacher Reverend Turk had alluded, and, therefore, offering proof positive that the Bible was indeed true. Crowds grew. The price to view the giant doubled to one dollar. Stagecoaches drawn by teams of four horses made the round trip from Syracuse and Rochester. The railroads started to schedule regular excursion trains all the way from New York City.

Two Yale professors, Othniel Marsh, an authority on fossils, and a chemist, Benjamin Sillman, meticulously examined the giant and declared him a true fossil.

James H. Drator from the New York State Museum, a distinguished paleontologist, disagreed. He thought the giant an ancient statue, proclaiming it, 'the most remarkable object yet brought to light in this country'.

There were dissenters. Doctor Andrew White, the first president of Cornell University, visited the site with a colleague who thought he detected chisel marks.

Erastus Dow Palmer, New York City's foremost sculptor, traveled to Cardiff on the railroad, and immediately declared fraud, saying the giant was neither fossil, nor statue, dismissing it as something 'planted,' maybe as lately as within the past year.

Meanwhile, at his museum and menagerie on Broadway in

New York City where he exhibited monstrosities such as living Canadian giants, fat girls, and a man without arms who could cut watch paper using his toes instead of fingers, Barnum was following the unraveling of all the mania. Always on the lookout for a good thing, he sent a representative to make his own assessment.

Barnum's agent arrived on a Sunday and witnessed incredibly in a six-hour stretch three thousand individuals view the stone man, each paying a dollar.

Barnum immediately made an offer either to buy or lease the giant. He was turned down.

Not to be deterred, he sent his own sculptor to Cardiff to study the remains, with orders to make him an exact duplicate of what he saw.

Within weeks, Barnum was exhibiting his own version of the giant at his museum on Broadway.

This was shortly before Christmas, and Hull, along with a syndicate he was now in business with, had had the idea to bring the giant down to Manhattan and reap the rewards of the holiday season.

Now, unfortunately, he found Barnum's hoax of his hoax outdrawing his real fake.

Hull went to court seeking an injunction against Barnum, but the judge, having heard all the controversy, declined to intervene or prohibit Barnum from exhibiting his fake of a fake.

No one suffered.

All the back and forth in the press only brought out larger and larger crowds more and more eager to view both specimens, and compare notes.

Opinions fell into four camps.

The first still held that the original Cardiff giant was an ancient fossil.

The second contended it a primitive sculpture.

The third sniffed at the whole affair, declaring it a hoax.

And the fourth opinion charged that the Barnum exhibition was in fact the real giant found buried at Cardiff while the one pretending to be the actual giant was in truth the fake.

Even eminences like Ralph Waldo Emerson and Oliver Wendell Holmes weighed in. Emerson visited and marveled that the giant was 'astonishing! . . . A bona fide, petrified human being.'

Dr. Holmes examined the giant minutely, even going so far as to bore a hole behind the petrified man's ear in search of an ancient fossilized brain. Finding nothing but rock, he declared the giant not a man, but a statue, 'probably of great antiquity'.

Following Holmes's lead, scientific opinion now firmly solidified on the side of ancient statue, but the press was not satisfied.

Journalists began nosing around.

The first real indication that all was not kosher was the curious detail that Hull's cousin, Farmer Stubby Newel, had spent the summer before the giant's discovery whining about how his well was about to dry up, but then after the discovery, nothing more was said about the well, and now it seemed fine, its water pure, plentiful, and free-running.

Add to this the fact that large amounts of currency had been flowing through Stubby's usually paltry bank account into the account of the cheap-cigar manufacturer George Hull, down at Binghamton.

Hull became the focus of the journalists' interest. It was learned that some months before, he had arrived in Syracuse with a large box marked MACHINERY. When asked about it, he claimed the machinery was ticketed for his tobacco factory, but workers there said no new piece of machinery had arrived at their manufactory for a good many years.

Now it was learned that Hull had been in Iowa, and his trade of a barrel of beer for a block of gypsum was soon uncovered.

The path of the heavy gypsum block along dirt roads and destroyed bridges was easy to follow, and in Chicago, under some threat to reveal their parts in a possible criminal investigation, the stonecutter and sculptor confessed.

So Hull's fabrication came wholly undone, and he was now quick to admit his part in it. He had done very well, he admitted. His end was more than a hundred thousand dollars.

Almost every paper in the country rushed to publish Hull's story.

But rather than destroy the profitability of the Cardiff Giant, lo and behold, the statue became even more popular as an attraction, as even larger crowds began to flock to see it, and the Barnum statue as well, validating what Barnum had been saying all along, that the public in no way minded being humbugged, as long as they were entertained at the same time they were being duped. And in some ways, here, in the hoax of the hoax, was the greatest delight.

Chapter Seventeen

In which Lozier, under pressure, finally agrees to set a
date for the work to begin.

NOW THE TIME was getting near where, more than ever, the
prospective workers were feeling the pressures of daily life
and waiting for the job to start. More and more were coming
around each day, hanging out and laughing, wondering
when everything would be set.

Lozier listened to them, taking joy in dealing with every
detail and trouble that they paraded in front of him.

He discussed the theory of sawing, the practicality of the
iron oarlocks, the tensile strength of the materials to be used.
The oars must be of a contiguous piece of wood, and there
was much discussion of where from ought these trees be
secured for maximum strength inherent to the wood fiber. A
hardwood such as ash would be ideal, and Lozier, the retired
carpenter, agreed, saying he already had his wood nymphs
out on the prowl in search of just so an arbor, that he had
spoken to a number of joiners, and the glue factory had
already begun their research for the perfect amalgam.

Several start-up dates were set, and then one after the
other delayed because Lozier was unhappy with the estimates
from the mechanics for the oars and towers.

In addition, wanting everything absolutely right, he stated
his uncertainty in regard to whether he had hired a large-
enough workforce, stressing his misgivings, but adamant that

he could not, and would not, given all the responsibility placed in his hands from the president of the United States to the mayor on down, go forward with a job of such magnitude, until he had hired sufficient numbers.

This led many of those who had already been engaged, fearful for their jobs if the project did not proceed, to seek out other possible workers over their own misgivings, each defensive of what they had and not wanting to give up any prospect, or prospective prospects even.

Pretty soon, with the heat of summer waning, it got so 'thick and pressing' with those poised and ready to get to work, anxious for the word, that Lozier was forced, finally, to 'name the day'.

He went away to 'contemplate', and came back saying he had given his plan careful, final thought. Under enormous pressure, he awarded the last contracts for the smithy work and for all outstanding supplies.

He went out of his way to not disappoint anyone and stressed this fact to the anxious assembled. He stated there was enough work and opportunity for all, and this remained his credo – to not favor a few, but to be equitable.

His good intention was applauded by everyone.

After careful consideration, he announced his intention to divide his workforce. His army was so large, they would need to proceed up to King's Bridge in two groups.

One group would meet at Bowery and Spring streets. The other at the fork where Broadway meets Bowery, at Fourteenth Street (near the site of Union Square today).

Chapter Eighteen

In which everything and nothing comes to a head.

ONLY LOZIER AND DE VOE FAILED TO SHOW.

The men began to arrive early, as they had been instructed. Some were carrying tools. Shovels, axes, picks. Some pushed wheelbarrows. Some came with their wives and children.

Contractors and carpenters drove up in wagons loaded with lumber and hammers and saws. Butchers drove herds of cattle and hogs, carts loaded with crated chickens.

At each site they were met by a fife-and-drum corps that had been engaged by Lozier to lead the army of workers on their triumphant trek north.

The atmosphere was jovial and full of hope.

On Bowery a man sat in a covered box, something like a seaside chair, with his feet up on a footstool, selling peanuts and apples from a table set out in front of him.

Nearby, another man, this one one-eyed, sold carefully wrapped wedges of maple-sugar coconut cake.

Not far away a fellow was bellowing, 'Tamaties! Tamaties! Git your love apples. Toe-may-toe figs! Tamaties! Tamaties!' trudging through the crowd, pulling a rickety wagon behind him, having little success, the luscious red fruit held to be poison.

Estimates were that between five hundred and a thousand workers had shown up at each locale.

They stood around for some time to no avail.

Finally after several hours, a contingent was sent back to Centre Market to see if either or both Lozier and De Voe could be located or to learn what had caused their delay.

At the market a message had been left. The message said that the pair had had to leave town, owing to matters of their health.

The messengers now returned to the Bowery with the news.

Word spread up to Fourteenth Street, and it didn't take long for the gathered there to march down and join their brothers and sisters.

For an hour the workers hung around wondering what to do, while the fife-and-drum bands continued on with their music.

The mood grew increasingly angry.

Gradually it dawned on more and more of them that they had been 'handsomely sold'. Cries went up for the police, for Old Hays. But what crime had been committed? Threats were muttered. The names Lozier and De Voe cursed.

Some, not wanting to appear fools, eventually began to back off, move away from standing with the others, situating themselves with the curious spectators who themselves had grown thick.

Very soon more stepped away. They began to jeer and berate those with whom they had only recently been standing. They in no way now wanted to be associated with, or desired to appear as if they had been 'engaged' in, the episode, and they began to heap ridicule upon the excited and angry ones who remained.

In the end, as the sun set, there were but a few who would in any way confess that they had signed on for the project to saw off Manhattan.

Final Chapter

In which we come to understand what transpired at the New York Historical Society when Uncle John De Voe met with his nephew the retired butcher and insecure author, Thomas Farrington De Voe, and try to piece together through research and speculation exactly what happened in the aftermath of that meeting.

ONE DAY somewhere between the years 1858 and 1860, Uncle John De Voe found his way to the New York Historical Society at the invitation of his nephew Thomas.

The striking, newly erected edifice stood on the southeast corner of Second Avenue at Eleventh Street. At that time Second Avenue was a broad and stately thoroughfare with handsome private residences, cool green parks, and solemn churches, extending up to Twentieth Street.

The Historical Society was a two-story building, done up in an Italian-Roman-Doric style, made from sandstone, with white-and-yellow pine floors laid over brick. The cost of construction was eighty-five thousand dollars. The architects had been Mettam and Burke. The cornerstone was laid October 17, 1855. In the judgment of the *Journal of Commerce*, it was a 'handsome, solid, and substantial' building.

The first floor was fully six feet above street level. Despite his rheumatism, Uncle John climbed the steps and entered the white-and-gold-tinted vestibule where the vaulted ceiling was supported by tall and graceful columns and there was impressive mosaic marble underfoot.

Through the open doors Uncle John could see into the lower galleries. Displayed was mostly portraiture, although his eye was caught by some fine and well-selected landscapes, still life of fruit, and game pieces.

He looked for his nephew and within a few moments spotted him coming down the stairway from above. They shook hands before Thomas took him by the elbow to lead him upstairs.

Here on the second floor was the quiet and subdued atmosphere of the reading rooms. Solemn, bespectacled old gentlemen, seated in cozy armchairs, seemed to be lost in the mysterious depths of huge folios and quartos, which were gray with age.

Nephew Thomas showed his uncle to the back of the room. 'Sit down, Uncle,' he said, guiding the old man into a horsehair stuffed leather seating chair. Now, under the cold, keen face of De Witt Clinton and the serene, clear forehead and piercing glance of Edgar Allan Poe, their conversation began.

By way of introduction, Thomas gave his elderly relative a brief history of the Historical Society. He told him that the institution had been founded in 1803 by De Witt Clinton, among others, indicating the portrait of the ex-mayor and governor, on the wall just above them. He went on to explain that this building in which they now sat was actually the Society's first permanent home. Before setting at this location the collection had been housed in one rental property after another.

The job of the Society was to collect and preserve all materials relating to the history of New York – books, newspapers, maps, journals, paintings, engravings et al.

Thomas told the story of how he had first been drawn here by his interest in all things military. This passion had been kindled when one day as a lad he had taken a walk with his grandmother on a tract of land known locally as 'Indian Field' in what is Van Cortlandt Park today in the Bronx, but at that time, when he was fourteen, encompassed the farm-lands of his great-uncles Frederick and Daniel De Voe.

Here, his grandmother told him, had been the site of a terrible massacre of brave Mohegan warriors, who had fought on the side of the Continental army, by British forces during the Revolution. Her gripping tale had left an indelible mark on the boy, and four years later, in 1829, at the age of eighteen, young Tom had joined the army, and from the day of his induction onward, his enthusiasm for the military had only grown.

After his army stint came to an end, he returned to the city and joined the family trade of butchery. He, along with some uncles and cousins, worked at the Jefferson Market, which at the time ranked among the best of the uptown markets. Here licenses were owned by several De Voes, including John De Voe, Sr. (with whom he now sat) in Stall No. 3, and his son, John De Voe, Jr. in Stall No. 6. In addition George W. De Voe, Frederick De Voe, Moses De Voe, and he, Thomas Farrington De Voe, worked in Stalls No. 5, 7, 8, and 10 respectively.

'But then day by day in my down hours from the market, I came to where the Society was then housed on Broadway, and began rummaging through the newspapers,' said Thomas, and at this point in his narration he rose to his feet and went to the shelf from which he brought back two large ledger books. These he opened and showed to his uncle. Here, in his meticulous, but nearly illegible hand lay a vast catalog of newspaper articles and assorted records that had caught his interest over the course of a decade of discriminate rummaging.

'Over the course of time, but especially since my retirement, I have been fortunate to become friends with George H. Moore, Esquire, the chief librarian here, a gentleman, esteemed, attentive, and obliging. Mr. Moore opened out to me all the rich treasures contained herein, and I eagerly *devoured*, not only the *military subjects*, but all connected with our city; and at last I began to *feel* that I had either swallowed or been bitten by a rabid antiquary.'

Librarian Moore eventually introduced De Voe as a member, and then one day had the presumption to suggest that he, De Voe, a common butcher by trade, prepare a paper, and address the Society in his own particular specialty. This was not the military as De Voe first thought, but the city market.

De Voe was astonished. At first skeptical of not only his ability to write, but also the value of anything that he might know, he engendered special fear at the prospect of addressing that august society insofar as his knowledge had any worth.

'But soon,' he told his uncle, 'I felt differently, as Mr. Moore made me see there is that historian, who in seeking his mental fare, looks only for the choicest and most substantial food to satisfy his natural appetite; and his eagle eye merely glances at the stray crumbs which have fallen from his plate, while the hungry gleaner, who follows after, is forced to pick them up, to cover such other rejected food as may be left, but which he gladly seizes and ravenously devours.'

After much apprehension, Thomas addressed the body on the evening of the May 4, 1858. 'On that date I read my paper before the New York Historical Society, and its reception was all, and more, than I expected; and if confession is proper here, I was elated – it struck in so deep!'

With the success of his paper, his friend and mentor now urged him to sally forth upon a book. In this important task he would ultimately be successful, although a planned second volume to include all markets in the United States outside of New York never came to fruition.

In the course of writing his book, De Voe undertook research, to speak to as many persons of his acquaintance as physically possible – other butchers, fishermen, farmers, purveyors, men and women with whom he had worked shoulder to shoulder, and some he was meeting for the first time.

'Permit me, Uncle,' he said, 'for this is what I have learned. Almost everyone, most especially the aged citizens of this city, have some special historical knowledge connected with family, friends, or neighborhood, worthy of being known and revealed for the instruction or gratification of others, or as shedding new light upon the annals of our city. Permit me to ask from you who have the power to grant it, to dwell upon your past, your own memories; if they be stirred by long-dormant recollections of remarkable incidents or scenes, they will be good enough to note these recollections, as material for my use, as I lay upon you what I hope will be the agreeable task of reviving bygone days in your mind's eye.'

Uncle John grunted, but was flattered. Here, later in life, it was nice to be needed. He and his nephew spent many days together, Uncle John regaling the young man with tales of things and people he recalled, butcher boys and hodmen, hucksters and forestallers and rowdies, Sam Way the shark catcher, oystermen and clam-men, idlers and vagabonds, chimney sweeps, garroters, and girls peddling radishes, plague sufferers, and massive oxen put on spits and grilled whole and served with cherry pie, Four Thieves Vinegar, and the Ship-bread Bakery where the bakers kneaded the dough with their feet. Then one day, well into his narrative, as Uncle John looked at the ledger on the reading table that contained the evidence of his curious nephew's many hours of scanning brittle old newspapers, . . . was it a glimmer that came into his dim eye, or a twinkle? He cracked a mostly toothless smile, folded his gnarled hands on his ample stomach, and pointed to the ledger, setting forth that it put him in mind of an incident not much known now but quite a to-do back then, and here he recalled a time and place at the old Centre Market and he regaled his nephew with the story of him and a man going by the name of Lozier and their escapades and the hoax of New York sawed in half.

Listening, Thomas laughed, and shook his head incredulously, as he took copious notes, enjoying himself thoroughly, for after all, if this was not history and its discovery, what was?

'And in the end what happened to Lozier, Uncle? I mean after it was all over,' Thomas asked when Uncle John had finished his tale.

'As I recall it,' chuckled Uncle John, 'he lay quietly housed up; and so he stayed several weeks, not daring to venture forth, and when he did so, he was disguised into the general appearance of a different person, and assumed his *proper* name; as some of the most excited had not only used hard words, but also threatened, if they ever got hold of Lozier, they would saw him off!'

Thomas was pleased to have such a wonderfully colorful story, and he never questioned it, including it in his *Market Book* in the chapter on Centre Market, just as he had been told it.

It was only later, well after the book was published and it was too late, when he was questioned by those who knew the market and had been around back then, and knew his Uncle John, that he came to realize that the old man's whole account was probably a load of hooey, and more than likely never ever occurred. He'd been handsomely sold.

Embarrassed and outraged, he was all the same stuck with it. There was nothing he could do. The worst of it was that he had been presumptuous enough to set off on the title page these words: *Fact, Not Fancy* Oh hubris! And woe to him! The ignominy of it all! He was compromised. His reputation, for what it was worth, was forever tarnished.

Or so he must have thought.

Over the years, long into history, others came to the Historical Society, or picked up Thomas Farrington De Voe's

Market Book, and read the story of 'New York Sawed in Half', and it tickled them, and they took note, and they retold it, and even elaborated on it, and some, even included it in their own books.

The great Asbury was the first. He told the tale as Chapter Eight in his illuminating *All Around the Town*, although the card catalog of the Historical Society qualifies that his account of 'Sawing Manhattan in Half' is 'an unreliable, embellished version'.

All the same, Alexander Klein saw nothing wrong with the account and chose to reprint that very version in his collection *Grand Deceptions: The World's Most Spectacular and Successful Hoaxes, Ruses, and Frauds*.

Chapter Seventeen of Edward Robb Ellis's *The Epic of New York City* is entitled 'Sawing Off Manhattan Island', and this, too, includes an account of the hoax drawn from De Voe's book. In his *Big Book of Hoaxes* crime encyclopediologist Carl Sifakis includes a graphic account of all the purported ministrations, which is skillfully illustrated by comic-book artist Rick Parker.

In none of the well-known personal accounts of the time is there mention of the incident: not in Dr. Charles Haswell's *Reminiscences of New York by an Octogenarian (1816–1860)*, not in Philip Hone's four-million-word diary, not in Grant Thorburn's vivid *Fifty Years' Reminiscences of New York; or, Flowers from the Garden of Laurie Todd*.

If there had been some mention of the hoax, one would think that De Voe's scrupulous newspaper research and indexing would have unearthed it.

De Voe's original ledger books remain extant in the stacks

at the New York Historical Society and still bear the plaques of their origin:

Slote & Janes
(Henry L. Slote and Jonathan Janes).
Stationers, Printers, and Blank Book
Manufacturers, Dealers in Foreign and
Domestic Stationery of Every Variety at
93 Fulton Street
near William Street.

Volume One begins with a notice from *The Flying Post*, a news sheet from Britain, dated August 13, 1696.

In this first ledger there are only two notations for the years in question. The first for 1823 mentions the first gas street-light company. The second, a citation for 1824, calls attention to the formation of the Society for Reformation of Juvenile Delinquents.

This first volume runs 411 pages in length.

Volume Two, beginning January 3, 1800, starts with a reference to an article on the death of George Washington culled from the *Daily Advertiser*.

According to Thomas De Voe, Uncle John, try as he may, couldn't remember, when recalling the hoax incident, whether it took place in 1823 or 1824.

Ledger notations for the year 1823 include articles from the *Commercial Advertiser*, the *New York American*, the *New York Gazette and General Advertiser*, and the *Evening Post*. There are references to steamboat arrivals, horse races, the formation of the gas company, a circus at Richmond Hill, a sketch of DeWitt Clinton, water for the city, a tiger in Kentucky, an account of the Negro Plot of 1712, balloon flights, reference to the New York Society for the Prevention of Pauperism, duels, an Egyptian mummy on exhibition in Boston, a prison ship anchored in the East River, a Greek ball, a plea for firemen wanted, the curious custom of Jewish weddings in Russia, cattle disease in Maryland, longevity among colored women, certain boxing matches, at least one murder, and a final tally of yellow-fever victims for the year.

For 1824 De Voe gives us illumination on more of the same, this time from the *National Advocate*, the *Commercial Advertiser*, and the *Evening Post*. Here, the chronicler's interest is caught by the state of the Horticultural Society, an account of convicts escaping from the treadmill at Bellevue, a dead man's body sold for his debts, a balloon in the shape of an elephant, and the fashionable drive to Haarlam. There is a description of markets in Washington, D.C., a deaf and dumb exhibition, and the still experimental trial of using leather to sheath ships. A whale was said to have swallowed a porpoise off the coast of Sandy Hook. The body of a young girl was stolen from her grave; a partridge flew into a woman's home and broke a looking glass; Johnny Edwards the scale-beam maker, the same Johnny Edwards who tried in vain to defend the slave Rose Butler from execution, this time managed to obtain a pardon for a convicted printer.

De Voe gave up his chore in 1850, 399 pages into this his second ledger.

No where in either of the ledgers is there a mention of the great hoax described to him by his uncle, although there is plenty to give exception to Asbury's argument that the press or its readership were entirely uninterested in the trials and tribulations of the lower classes, and therefore, the incident was passed over or never even recognized as anything.

Upon learning that he had been humbugged by his own uncle, Thomas was shattered, humiliated, devastated. Already he was insecure enough to continually preface his work with apology upon apology, each acknowledging his insecurity and unworthiness, even lamely defending *his* right to write, being a lowly butcher and no author: 'In my case, being found here, so much out of *my line*, I must therefore leave the reader to judge, and determine my position from his own estimate of my merit.'

Fact, Not Fancy.

There is no mollification. We can only imagine the man's mortification in being so compromised.

Did Thomas De Voe, the author, spend the rest of his life looking for a way to get even with his own blood relative?

Yes or no, the chance came.

After spending long years casting about for a fitting subject for another substantial project, a fitting follow-up to the market book, he eventually settled on his own family.

A Genealogy of the de Veaux (De Voe, Devoe, etc. etc.) Family, Commencing with the first of the name found in various early records, dating back above eleven hundred years ago saw print in 1885. The book is an octavo, three hundred pages in length, with separate index and appendix.

The De Voe family turns out to be Huguenots, French Protestants who fled under persecution from France to Mannheim, Germany, before immigrating to America.

Poring through old newspapers, books, documents of various kinds, as well as traditional accounts, Thomas lists twenty-five variations he uncovered of the name De Voe. These include De Voe, DeVoe, Devoe, De Veau, de Veaux, de Vaux, De Vaulk, Devorax, Devoues, Davaux, De Vos, Devoor, Du Four, Devoer, Devoier, De Voo, Du Vou, De Voue, De Voose, Devooise, De Vooe, Dye Vou, Da Vouce, Da Veau, and finally, Davoue.

Within the three hundred pages, are thousands of listings of extended-family members. There are no less than eighty-nine John De Voes, or variants thereof, listed.

John De Voe. Mother was Hester See. Became a member of the Old Sleepy Hollow Church.

John De Voe, resided in New Paltz, then moved to Vermont.

John De Voe, born in 1756, and was just 19 when the Revolution began. Fond of firing his musket at British warships as they passed on the North River. When the gunboats trained their armament and fired back, he would shout, 'Down, boys!' at his companions as warning for them to duck. Married during the war.

John De Voe, born 1785. Noncommissioned officer during the War of 1812.

John De Voe, born 1807, died quite young.

John De Voe, engaged in raising products for the New York markets, which were conveyed in small sailing vessels and rowboats to the city.

John De Voe, steamship captain, piloting the propeller *Chester* from New Rochelle to New York and back.

John De Voe, a sculptor. Also in the stonecutting business.

John De Voe, engaged in wool-carding and cloth-dressing.

John De Voe, struck down during the Revolution by a heavy sword cut that rendered him senseless, and left him with lifelong pain, along with an indented forehead, made by the musket stock that Captain Drake drove into his brain.

John De Voe, a private.

John De Voe, a captain.

John De Voe, a mariner.

John De Voe, a rigger.

John De Voe, a turner.

John De Voe, a ship's carpenter.

John De Voe, a dock builder.

John De Voe, a mason.

John De Voe, a wheelwright.

John De Voe, a bookbinder.

John De Voe, a clerk.

John De Voe, an insurancer.

John De Voe, died of yellow fever on Mott Street, New York City.

John De Voe, died of measles.

John De Voe, died suddenly while at work on the fortifications near New York in 1814.

John De Voe, died young, from fright.

John De Voe, killed in the Rebellion.

But no mention, at least identifiable, of Uncle John De Voe, the butcher from the Jefferson Market, Uncle John De Voe, the charlatan, the hoaxer, the humbugger. Uncle John De Voe, the man who had set up his own nephew, pulled his coat, sold him handsomely, embellishing on what had probably been a small joke one sunny day at the Centre

Market, if that, making it into a hoax of a hoax, sawing New York in half, blatantly flimflamming his own flesh and blood.

So here is final revenge, perpetrated not in Butcher Samuel Winship's Bunker Hill bullbaiting ring, but in the arena of the New York Historical Society, as wronged nephew, Thomas Farrington De Voe (1811–1892), took opportunity to exact it. Because, by all evidence from the De Voe family genealogy, it seems that Uncle John, the irascible, the diddler, the hoaxer, the humbugger has effectively, and neatly, been sawed off the family tree.

End Word

THE FIRST TIME I encountered the story of Lozier and Uncle John De Voe and their skullduggery was when I read an excerpt from Thomas De Voe's *The Market Book* in *New York City Folklore* by B.A. Botkin.

I was intrigued and tickled from the start, and shortly after came across another version, much embellished and even more satisfying, in Herbert Ashbury's *All Around the Town*, and then still another telling in Edward Robert Ellis' *The Epic of New York City*.

When I began *New York Sawed in Half*, I anticipated going into newspaper archives, poring over diaries, journals, letters, and other first-hand accounts, to learn even more of Lozier and De Voe's wonderful hoax, and its impact on the naïve and unsuspecting participants.

No such luck.

In the end, I found all roads led back to that one single mention in Thomas De Voe's book. As I dug deeper, and spoke to more and more people (librarians at the New York Historical Society and the New York Public Library, curators at the Museum of the City of New York, and learned local historians) it became exceedingly apparent that this whimsical tale may very well never have happened at all.

My first despairing thought was to abandon the project. The hoax may have never occurred, and, therefore, deserved no further notice. But then speaking further to those very same librarians and other New York historians, it became evident that the hoax's authenticity no longer mattered. The story was part of the fabric of the city's history, as much as Washington Irving's Diedrich Knickerbocker, and Asbury's own gangs of New York, and against a context of nineteenth century ruse, hoax, and humbug, it was important.

So as Asbury has embellished his story, I have followed suit, even further conjuring what might have been. I have imagined numerous scenes wholly, and put words in Lozier and Uncle John's mouths. I have drawn heavily for this purpose from Thomas De Voe's remarkable work, attributing anecdotes and stories to Uncle John. As I imagine it, many of them found there way into Thomas's book through tales told by his uncle.

This book is not meant as one of historical scholarship. It is what I hope to be an entertainment, a reimagining of a piece of the past that may well have been imagined in the first place; it remains, nevertheless, one of the stories that makes up the very colorful history of a great city.

Joel Rose
New York City
November, 2000

Bibliography

All Around the Town by Herbert Asbury.

American Notes for General Circulation by Charles Dickens.

American Renaissance: Art and Expression in the Age of Emerson and Whitman by F. O. Matthiessen.

Beneath the American Renaissance by David S. Reynolds.

The Big Book of Hoaxes with other writers and illustrated by various artists by Carl Sifakis.

The Book of New York by Robert Shackleton.

The Collected Tales and Poems of Edgar Allan Poe

The Columbia Historical Portrait of New York by John A. Kouwenhoven.

The Diary of Philip Hone (1828–1851) by Philip Hone.

Domestic Manners of the Americans by Frances Trollope.

The Double Dealers: Adventures in Grand Deception by Alexander L. Klein. ed.

Dynasty: The Astors and their Times by David Sinclair.

Edgar A. Poe: Mournful and Never-ending Remembrance by Kenneth Silverman.

The Encyclopedia of New York City, Kenneth T. Jackson. ed.

The Epic of New York City by Edward Robb Ellis.

Fifty Years' Reminiscences of New York; or, Flowers from the Garden of Laurie Todd by Grant Thorburn.

Gotham: A History of New York City to 1898 by Edwin G. Burrows and Mike Wallace.

Grand Deception, Alexander Klein. ed.

The Great Riots of New York: (1712–1873) by Joel Tyler Headley.

The Gangs of New York by Herbert Asbury.

A History of New York by Diedrich Knickerbocker by Washington Irving.

Hot Corn: Life Scenes in New York by Solon Robinson.

Infamous Manhattan by Andrew Roth.

Israfel: The Life and Times of Edgar Allan Poe by Hervey Allen.

Low Life: Lures and Snares of Old New York by Luc Sante.

The Market Book, containing a Historical Account of the Public Markets in the Cities of New York, Boston, Philadelphia, and Brooklyn, with a Brief Description of Every Article of Human Food Sold Therein, the Introduction of Cattle in America, and Notices of Many Remarkable Specimens by Thomas F. De Voe.

Martin Chuzzlewit by Charles Dickens.

The Mysterious Death of Mary Rogers: Sex and Culture in Nineteenth Century New York by Amy Gilman Srebnick.

New York City Cartmen, 1667–1850 by Graham Russell Hodges.

New York City Folklore, B.A. Botkin. ed.

The New York Tombs: Its Secrets and Its Mysteries by Charles Sutton.

A People's History of the United States by Howard Zinn.

Poverty in New York (1783–1825) by Raymond A. Mohl.

P. T. Barnum: America's Greatest Showman by Philip B. Kunhardt., Jr., Philip B. Kunhardt III, and Peter W. Kunhardt

Reminiscences of a New York Octogenarian (1816–1860) by Charles Haswell.

Struggles and Triumphs by P. T. Barnum.

Sunshine and Shadow in New York by Matthew Hale Smith.

The Unabridged Edgar Allan Poe by Tam Mossman.

Valentine's Manual of the City of New York for 1916–7 by Henry Collins Brown.

Valentine's Manual of the City of New York 1917–1918 by Henry Collins Brown.

Water for Gotham by Gerard T. Koeppel.

What I Saw in New York: or a Bird's Eye View of City Life by Joel H., M. D. Ross.

A Note on the Author

Joel Rose is the editor of the Urban Historicals series.
He is the author of the novels *Kill the Poor* and
Kill Kill Faster Faster. He founded the literary
magazine *Between C&D* and has edited
several literal anthologies.